Decorate This, Not That!

Dedication

For Sun, wherever your star may be shining.

First published in 2018 by

G Arts
600 Third Avenue
New York, NY 10016

www.gartsbooks.com
media@gartsbooks.com

First edition, 2018

Library of Congress Cataloging-in-Publication data is available from the publisher.

Design: Liz Trovato

Hardcover edition
ISBN: 978-0-9987474-3-9

Printed and bound in China

10 9 8 7 6 5 4 3 2 1

Floor Plan Illustrations by Linda Stehno
64: Britney Jette, *In the Garden*
pg. 40: San Diego History Center, *Chicken of the Sea–Woman Holding Tuna 1931*

Decorate This, Not That!

Janet Lee

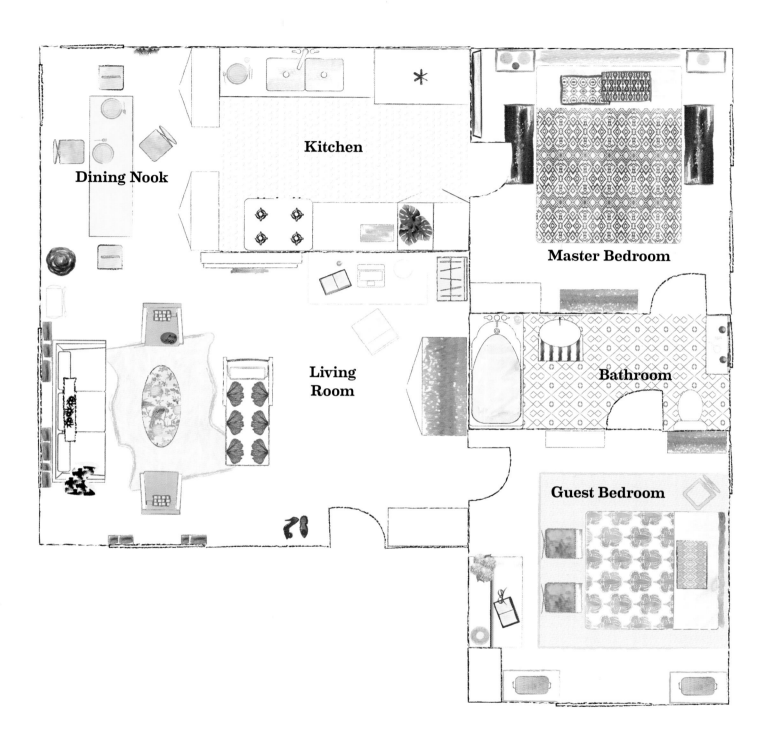

Dining Nook

Kitchen

Master Bedroom

Living
Room

Bathroom

Guest Bedroom

Introduction

Jim Blandings: What's this, another closet?

Muriel Blandings: This happens to be our living room. This isn't it...

Jim Blandings: Maybe it's this little room...?

Muriel Blandings: That's the powder room.

Jim Blandings: Just where is the dining room?

Muriel Blandings: It was right here a minute ago.

Jim Blandings: We couldn't just have lost it!

Mr. Blandings Builds His Dream House, 1948

For this two-decades-strong, self-anointed blue-ribbon serial small-space nester firmly rooted in New York City, it was time to hit the road again. This time all signs were pointing west, back to my hometown in sunny Southern California to be closer to family. Along with my furry four-legged pal, I would be packing up memories of over a dozen diminutive digs—measuring no more than 800 square feet on a good day—emboldened by a list of tried-and-true space-maximizing tips and sneaky design fixes that have guided me like the North Star in each petite habitat to live large, happy, and proud. Keeping décor and storage ideas smart and affordable yet posh and portable has become the core of the *Decorate This, Not That!* manifesto.

I was to inherit a run-down beach house built in the 1940s, all 614 square feet of it, blessed with good bones and a prime location, just a few short blocks from the Pacific Ocean. Sadly neglected over the years as a rental property, this petite pad looked more shack than cozy cottage. The former front lawn had lost its battle long ago between aggressive weed clusters and years of drought, hinting to the patched-up and faded décor inside. The stained wall-to-wall carpeting in the living room and bedrooms, mismatched wood paneling in the kitchenette, and caught-in-a-time-warp floor tiles in the bathroom put any fantasy of an easy, breezy beach retreat on pause.

And as I watched the movers unload the contents of my New York City apartment under a palm tree—while surfers straight from Central Casting walked past the front garden gate—it was also clear that my urban New York design sensibility was about to turn on its head. My penchant for dark, saturated wall colors, leather chairs, and heavy shantung drapes would no longer work in this sun-filled home by the shore. But moving into a new *nutshell* does not mean starting with a clean design slate. This is *real-world* decorating, which requires repurposing, painting, sewing, resurfacing, as well as upcycling furniture and lighting in new and fresh, space-enhancing ways. Fans of my blog will be able to play a game of Where's Waldo with my old sofa, desk, chairs, picture frames, and art. What room will they end up in next?

The overall game plan was to upgrade the cottage while I lived there, with the intention of flipping it back as a rental property in a few years' time. Because this cottage was not going to be a forever home, the *Decorate This, Not That!* noncommittal style standard was really put through its paces: keeping décor, furniture, and storage chic, unique, multifunctional, penny-wise, and versatile enough to take with me to the next abode.

In fact, the renovation of this mini beach bungalow, affectionately known as my home *du jour*, ushered in a separate category of décor I call *for-the-moment* fixes: ad hoc design solutions that are practical, easy on the wallet, a cinch to install yourself, and that still maintain a chic profile. In the kitchen, for instance, the tacky floor tiles will eventually be demolished and replaced, but an affordable, stylish, repurposable for-the-moment fix saved the day: removable and reusable rubber garage tiles that click into place without adhesives.

In this cottage and in each humble habitat I've called home, I've tried to ward off the dreaded three Cs of small-space decorating:

clutter, claustrophobia, and cookie-cutter design. The antidote to all three evils is to put a custom twist on the majority of the storage, lighting, and accessories used in the space. Whether it's revamping worn-out leather chairs with paint or upcycling a laundry cart into a Hollywood Regency bar on wheels, using accessible materials in chic, surprising, and multifunctional ways helps to elevate a shrunken floor plan so it lives and breathes like a grander, well-appointed home. Clever furniture, décor, and storage hacks with a strong *Make-It-Yourself* attitude are the backbone of this book and are represented as *MIY* projects in each chapter. The projects are ranked with clock icons (one clock = one hour or less, two clocks = two to five hours, three clocks = six-plus hours) to help gauge the time commitment involved. Also, to keep you on budget, dollar sign icons (one dollar icon = $50 or less, two dollar icons = $100 or less, three dollar icons = $500 or less) are attached to each project so you can decide where and where not to spend your valuable time and resources.

Here are the *Decorate This, Not That!* mantras that keep me on track, on budget, and energized:

☞ From limitations comes creativity. Being short on square inches and confined by a tight décor budget will drive the discovery of ingenious design solutions for your petite home. Remember, flaws can be your friend.

☞ Living small is not a mandate for subdued color palettes, patterns, and sparse furniture layouts. Go bold with color, and layer, layer, layer. Surround yourself with things you love. Let your maximalist flag fly!

☞ A handmade home is a happy home. Whether it's gluing trim to a curtain or painting stripes on a wall, custom touches along with one-of-a-kind handcrafted art and vintage pieces infuse a pocket-sized flat with a sense of history, personality, and unique character that starts to tell your story. Personality trumps square inches every time.

CHAPTER 1

Lofty Living

> "What are four walls, anyway? They are what they contain. The house protects the dreamer. Unthinkably good things can happen, even late in the game. It's such a surprise."
>
> — Frances Mayes, *Under the Tuscan Sun*

As a matter of survival in each of my dozen paltry-sized pads, the living room has had to quickly adopt multiple personalities. By day, it steps up as a bustling home office with the phone, printer, scanner, and computer all at arm's length, or it doubles as an impromptu craft, sewing, and paint workshop. By night, it may morph into a bedroom (flashing back to those studio apartment days) or a cozy movie and cocktail lounge.

But at first glance, this 187-square-foot living room, typical of older homes built in the 1940s, seemed to have only one personality: boxed in. Open floor plans are a modern notion, and a 25-inch-wide wall partition blocking the living room from the dining nook was

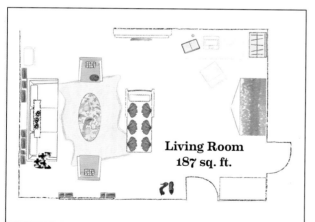

**Living Room
187 sq. ft.**

an annoying relic from the past, standing in the way of total sun-filled bliss. For a few hundred dollars, the wall was removed (the only demolition involved in this entire cottage makeover), and now the open layout allows natural sunlight to envelop both rooms, creating more usable living space with the same amount of square footage. Finally, my full-size New York sofa could squeeze into place!

Once the stained carpeting was removed, work and play zones could be defined with art, plants, lighting, and color, creating key focal points that keep a vertically and horizontally challenged space from feeling and functioning like a cramped cubbyhole. In this chapter, everything from furniture placement and paint color to window treatments and clever storage ideas will help your living room live larger and function smarter.

Roll up your sleeves! Here's the *Decorate This, Not That!* insider list for maximizing your space, storage, time, and budget, all while minimizing flaws in a snug living room.

Room Dreams

Before wall removal...

...after wall removal

BEFORE

AFTER

Decorate and unify adjoining spaces with a pared-back palette, compartmentalize rooms with contrasting shades.

In this open floor plan, keeping a tight color palette creates a calm cohesiveness in narrow confines. The overall cool, pale blue-gray shade helps the eye travel effortlessly between the living room and dining nook, which visually reads as one large airy space. Remember, when used on walls, lighter and cooler shades on the color wheel—like greens, blues, violet, and some grays—help make the surface appear to recede (or move away from you) and can have an expansive visual impact.

tip 👉 *On the back of a paint chip card, there is a Light Reflectance Value or LRV number assigned to each shade. From a scale of 0 (absorbs all light) to 100 (reflects all light colors), an LRV number higher than 50 percent will reflect more light back into the room than is absorbed into the walls, amplifying the look of cramped quarters. In this space, Sherwin-Williams' Rarified Air paint color (with 20 percent more blue added) has a high LRV rating of 76. It makes the front room of this cottage light, bright, and airy.*

Decorate and keep the flooring continuous, **chop up the eyeline in cramped quarters.**

Maintaining the same flooring material throughout the living room and the dining area imparts a sense of expansiveness and alludes to spaces beyond the room's four walls. In this case, there was enough money in the budget to lay down hand-scraped laminate flooring in the living and dining room for a cohesive, flowing look and function. You can create the same design harmony using similar-colored rugs or flexible modular carpet tiles.

Decorate and stage furniture toward the center of the living room, **lined up against the wall like a waiting room at the DMV!**

When hard-pressed for square footage, the knee-jerk reaction is to push sofas, chairs, and lighting as close to the wall as possible in an attempt to economize space. But if you can't see the edges of the room, you tend to perceive the space as tinier than it actually is. The better approach is to pull furniture off the wall (even a few inches helps) for some breathing room and to group pieces closer together based on similar function. Floating furniture toward the center of the room ups the cozy factor and creates an illusion of greater depth and a larger floor plan.

Decorate with a rug large enough to layer under the front legs of the sofa and chairs, a throw rug that only anchors the coffee table.

Letting the rug run beneath the furniture fools the eye into believing that the rug continues indefinitely, thereby making your space appear roomier.

A beloved shearling rug that once decorated my tiny New York bedroom looked fresh and new in the California sun-filled living room but was not large enough to anchor the entire seating arrangement. The petite shearling alone visually dwarfed the look of the room. A budget-friendly solution is to layer a small, low-pile, shaved shearling under the original rug, combining different textures of the same material to expand the look of the flooring. Positioned at a slight angle, the two rugs touch and tuck under most of the seating in the space. The difference in rug textures also brings depth to the sitting area without being distracting.

tip ☞ *Sometimes it is cheaper to buy two identical rugs in a smaller size than one large one. You can connect two rugs with strong carpet seaming tape made for this exact purpose. Attach on the back of the adjoining seam of each rug.*

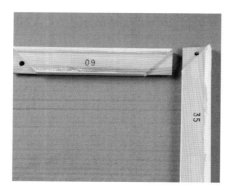  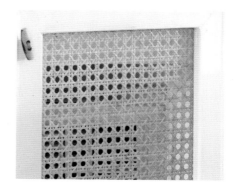

Leave the front of the heater uncovered, or you can make two custom cabinet doors using inexpensive wooden artist stretcher bars (available in a variety of sizes) for the frames and chair caning for the door fronts. Simply click the wooden frame together at the mitered corners. Staple the corners for a secure hold from underneath. Next, for easy pliability, soak caning in warm water for ten minutes in a bathtub. Lightly pat dry, measure, and cut to size with craft scissors. Next, use a staple gun to attach caning to the back of each frame. Add hinges and attach to the shelving unit for a custom radiator cover, complete with bonus storage to boot. For a simple closure, drill two small holes on the front sides of each cabinet panel 1½ inches from the top edge and ¼ inch from the center. In one hole, thread through a wood toggle (found at sewing stores) with a suede cord, and in the adjoining hole, tie the suede cord into a loop for the toggle to slip through.

tip 👉 *In order to accommodate the depth of your heater or air conditioner, the étagère may need to stand a few inches away from the wall. This extra space also allows for hot air to circulate freely. For added stability, secure the top of the shelving to the wall with an adhesive Velcro furniture strap, and screw the other end into the wall. It is easy to install and hard to detect.*

Decorate with a mash-up of vintage and modern for a dimension-boosting contrast, *not* order furniture sets straight from a catalog.

In a jam-packed room short on natural focal points, design contrast plays up the illusion of depth and dimension and wards off the deadly small-space decorating sins of being tiny—and boring. Pairing this vintage chaise longue with a funky, pop art printed tablecloth-turned-slipcover in bright Kelly green, imparts a fresh vitality to this living room, shifting the attention away from its meager proportions.

tip ☞ *For no-sew slipcovers conveniently sized to fit small benches, ottomans, or a chaise longue, shop in the kitchen bargain department for tablecloths, more readily available in large modern prints than at your local fabric store. Plus, the finished sewn edges offer more no-sew style possibilities. Attach under the cushion with sheet straps to keep fabric tucked in place without any damage to the fibers.*

Decorate and shop in the kids' department for designer look-alike lighting for less, **pay full *grown-up* prices.**

A wooden-beaded chandelier like this one, featured in a kids' home décor catalog, can be 25 to 30 percent cheaper than one from a regular home department. Small-space dwellers often think they don't have enough real estate to display a chandelier properly, but the opposite is true. Hanging a chandelier draws the eye upward, creating the perception of more vertical space. This chandelier also adds a touch of relaxed glamour to the beach bungalow.

Decorate big, *not* puny.

Tip the scale in favor of supersized anchor pieces like a desk or a lamp, which become the bold gestures that make a sparse room appear grand instead of apologetic. A large, six-foot-long glass desk establishes the work zone without encroaching on the rest of the living room, thanks to its clear profile. Paired with an oversized see-through acrylic lamp, chair, and MIY file cabinet on wheels (see MIY Project on the next page), this work corner looks and feels open and airy.

p.s. *Negotiating snug spots is never without a few decorating bumps along the way. Because this petite cottage only offers one wall long enough to accommodate the desk, one corner of it overlaps the front of fireplace mantel by a few inches. Thankfully, because it is clear glass, the flaw is not an eyesore. One important lesson is learned: mastering small-space living is all about improvising and letting go of perfection.*

miy PROJECT

Adding clear caster wheels to the bottom of an acrylic magazine rack gives it a get-up-and-go advantage as a mini rolling file cabinet, perfect for pared-down home office needs. Use a piece of masking tape on both sides of where you want to drill and use a sharp diamond drill bit to reduce the possibility of splitting the acrylic. Accessorize and stack the top of the cart with a see-through tray, stapler, and tape dispenser. Clear rubber furniture pads attached to the bottom of trays and boxes keep them from shifting.

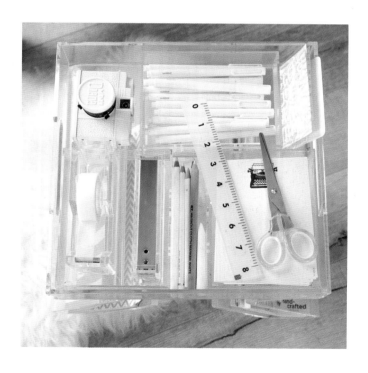

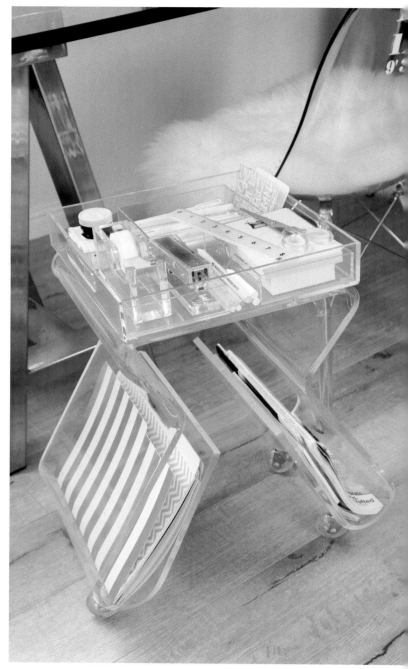

tip 👉 *Cozy up an office nook by personalizing the back of a clear, acrylic chair with custom GPS coordinates of your little nest. Removable adhesive decals, printed in matte white, can be ordered for the price of a large caramel macchiato.*

Decorate and declutter a narrow bookshelf with a unifying color theme, **not** let collectibles run amok.

In this tight corner, the narrow built-in bookshelf stands as the face of the home office. Lining the shelf with hand-painted gift wrap, accented with brushstrokes of gold on cream creates a backdrop of calm, while reds and browns allow personal photos and memorabilia to stand out as a collection, not clutter.

tip ☞ *Humble art, like my father's sweet sketches, gains prominence framed in a large white mat. Choose a picture frame that is double the size of your image for maximum style impact.*

**Decorate and slipcover a
run-of-the-mill faux fireplace
into the star attraction,**

let it fade into the background.

Working or not, a fireplace is a gift from the heavens when you live in a little lair, but left to its original white-on-white façade, this featureless fireplace disappeared into the wall. To give this faux fireplace some architectural oomph without committing to paint or tile, affordable artist canvas was customized into a no-sew slipcover. Vintage images of twigs, branches, and acorns were easily photo-transferred onto the canvas using a computer printer and artist gel medium. Now the eye is immediately drawn to the fireplace, drawing attention away from the room's shortcomings.

tip  *See Resource Guide for a list of free downloadable clip art.*

miy PROJECT

Buy primed artist canvas on a roll, available in extra-wide widths at better art supply stores, to cover an entire fireplace mantel in one solid piece. Measure and cut a paper pattern according to the width, height, and depth of your fireplace façade using brown craft paper. Tape the pattern to the canvas and cut out the slipcover shape. Print images according to your design theme with a laser printer found at a local printing shop on regular 20-pound weight paper stock. A home inkjet printer won't work for this project because the ink will start to run once it touches the gel transfer medium.

Cut out laser prints so they are bordered by a little bit of white paper. Paint a generous layer of artist soft gel medium (available at art and craft stores) directly onto the canvas, large enough to cover the size of the image. Then paint a gel layer onto the front of the laser-printed image. Place the image front side down onto the gel-primed canvas and smooth out any bubbles. Use a damp paper towel to wipe off any excess that may spill outside the edges. If you make a mistake or if images aren't aligning the way you'd like, immediately take a damp cloth and wipe off the image. You have a ten-minute window before it becomes too difficult to remove the image cleanly. Once you are happy with the composition of images, let dry for an hour or two.

Once dried, take a damp sponge and moisten the back of the glued laser images. Gently peel off the top paper layer, leaving the transferred image intact and affixed to the canvas. Saturate the surface again with water and carefully use your fingers to rub off the excess paper pulp, leaving a cleanly transferred image behind. Let dry for fifteen minutes, and repeat if there is remaining paper pulp. Hang your fireplace slipcover using a few strips of double-stick carpet tape and some small upholstery tacks. When it's time for a new look or moving day, roll up the canvas and hit the road!

Decorate and entice with a depth-alluding herringbone pattern,

not

leave a faux fireplace without natural wood elements.

Natural materials like wood instantly add warmth and texture to a sparse room, and they give this nonworking fireplace just enough pattern and a touch of drama to draw the eye in. Using a herringbone pattern, like this one made from wood Popsicle sticks, is a trick designers rely on to enhance the perception of size in a narrow room or nook. The eye tends to look at the wide Vs, which are created by the opposing wood sticks. When arranged horizontally across, they can make a niche appear wider than it really is.

tip 👉 *Dressing up the mantel with a jumbo wood garland plays with the scale of its modest proportions.*

*miy*PROJECT

To keep the design flexible and portable, foam core boards are cut to fit over the three interior walls of the mantel. Rub wood stain (varying shades of brown or gray) onto inexpensive wood craft or Popsicle sticks. Let dry. With a ruler and pencil, divide the boards into even portions horizontally and vertically, creating a grid based on the length of your wood strips. This will be your guide to lay out the herringbone pattern correctly.

Cut wood pieces with craft scissors to size, and then glue them into a herringbone pattern directly onto the boards, using a protractor to position wood strips at 45-degree angles from the center vertical line. There will be some wood strips that hang over the edges of the boards. Let the glue dry, and then use a straight edge and a craft knife to trim the excess wood to be even with the top, bottom, and sides. Pop boards securely into place using a few strips of carpet tape. Brilliant!

Decorate and exhibit local archive photos that give a sparse home provenance and a sense of history,

waste money on soulless poster art.

Art and photography prints can add to the design integrity of a teeny space short on character, especially if they're rooted in the city or neighborhood where you live. High-quality prints can get pricey, but look no further than your local public library or historical society for access to a rare photo collection unique to your own town, priced to fit any budget. Many local archive centers offer medium- to jumbo-sized prints, even including gallery-wrapped canvas framing options. Sale proceeds go toward the preservation of the archives, so it's art with a purpose.

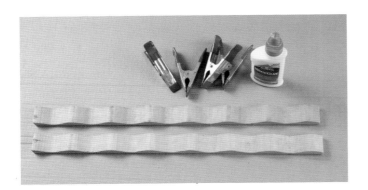

*miy*PROJECT

Cut two strips of inexpensive wood wiggle molding, found at any hardware store, about four inches wider than your print so there is nice selvage on each side to play with. Apply wood glue along the straight edges to create one solid scalloped wood strip. Paint the wood strip, and glue metal office clips onto the front. Removable adhesive strips keep your new revolving gallery frame secure on the wall.

Decorate and designate a cramped corner as a full-service bar and beverage zone, *not* with just a one-trick-pony end table.

A mini-cart on wheels is an adaptable small-space décor staple that I've come to rely on in each of my dinky digs. Being able to move things around makes you feel less beholden and locked in. This former laundry cart stands in seamlessly as a portable bar and beverage station while also pitching in as an end table. It can even be wheeled outside for garden cocktail parties. *Have bar, will travel!* Ice buckets and a large collection of stemware are stored out in the open for easy access and self-serve entertaining, and as a perk, they free up precious kitchen cabinet space. The little cocktail cart also has the *big* job of establishing a visual separation between the living room and the dining nook, preventing what I call "shoebox syndrome." With established zones, a dimensionless cubby of a space lives and breathes like a grander home.

tip 👉 *Hang a gold bathroom caddy on the side of the bar cart and guests will have an extra spot to rest a cocktail.*

tip 👉 *Maximize the sparkle in your petite nook. Line cart shelves with custom-cut mirrors. This is an affordable designer touch with a priceless payoff, reflecting light and a hint of glamour into a crowded corner. Most glass and mirror vendors will cut while you wait.*

Decorate and *fake* a foyer
where none exists,

not

physically block the flow
of the entryway.

In many tiny abodes like this cottage,
the front door skips straight ahead into
the living room. To ease that living-
in-a-cubicle feel, create a welcoming
pause between the doorway and the
living room with a faux foyer. Anchor
a scaled-down entryway vignette
with a skinny console table, a mirror,
light sconce, or wall art that functions
as a proper foyer where keys, gloves,
and mail are dropped, sorted, and
organized.

Decorate with freestanding shelving, *not* tables or storage units with bulky legs.

Floor space is at a premium in a minuscule maison. A simple gold lacquer tray turned foyer shelf is slim enough to hold its own as an ideal catchall for keys and mail, without cluttering the entryway. With only 18 inches of width and 14 inches of depth to play with, this freestanding shelf also opens up the floor for a shoe basket to tuck underneath without obstructing the door. Keep an eye out for shelf brackets that offer a bonus layer of storage for outgoing packages or even an umbrella.

tip ☛ *For shelving brackets on the go, minimize damage to the wall by using Wall-Dog screws that fasten directly into drywall without an anchor. Simply remove screws, then patch small holes and paint when you move on to greener pastures.*

Decorate and fortify a junior foyer with a double-layer shoe basket,

not

with storage solutions too fussy to maintain.

In cramped quarters, you have to be vigilant about clutter control, but it's so easy to set up organizational systems that are too lofty and don't cater to how you actually use the space. Growing up in an Asian household where shoes are removed at the door, the front entryway starts to look like a locker room without a simple storage system. To avoid the inevitable shoe pileup, tuck a small round basket inside a slightly larger one to create the right amount of storage structure and keep wayward *soles* upright and corralled.

*miy*PROJECT

Place a small round basket inside the center of a slightly wider and taller one that has a 2½- to 3-inch interior space between the two. Secure both baskets together from the bottom using twine or plastic cable ties.

tip ☞ *Keep your shoe basket marvelously mobile. Place the basket on a plastic plant dolly with wheels (easily painted to match your décor). The dolly will collect any dirt or moisture from shoes and is easy to wipe clean. The basket also easily wheels out of the way when you need to clean or clear the dance floor!*

Decorate snug spots with light sconces,

 not

space-monopolizing floor lamps.

A light sconce hanging from the wall elegantly establishes this makeshift foyer while leaving floor space free and clear. To keep lighting portable, simply change the cord to a plug-in (easy conversion kits are available at hardware stores). This broken sconce was collecting dust in my family's garage, and instead of paying to rewire it, the lamp was wrapped with plug-in patio lights.

tip ☞ *Spray-paint the lamp cord gold (remember to tape off the light socket openings) to blend in with the sconce, and attach it to a plug-in dimmer for full control at your fingertips.*

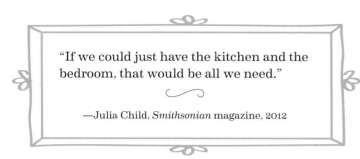

Standing

> "If we could just have the kitchen and the bedroom, that would be all we need."
>
> —Julia Child, *Smithsonian* magazine, 2012

In any other setting, the words "standing room only" conjure up some cool, *selfie-worthy* memories: rocking out front row at a sold-out concert or balancing martini glasses through the crowd at the hottest bar opening in town. But in this neglected, worn-down galley kitchen—all 74 square feet of it—standing and quickly passing through were the only things you wanted to do. It didn't help that there were no windows in the kitchen and that the door to the master bedroom was only inches away from the refrigerator. I took a deep breath and channeled the famous words of Julia Child: "If you're afraid of butter, use cream," a quote that graced the chalkboard wall in my New York City kitchen for years. The same scrappy, can-do spirit Ms. Child had toward cooking, I try to embrace toward small-space design—with far fewer calories! Making the best of what you have, improvising along the way, knowing that there are very few decorating mistakes that can't be rectified with a little paint and Spackle, gives you the push forward to experiment and discover innovative solutions to your unique small-space challenges.

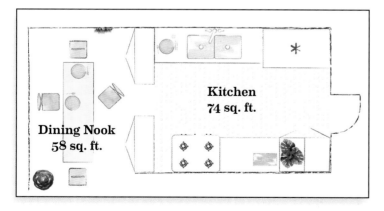

Kitchen
74 sq. ft.

Dining Nook
58 sq. ft.

At second glance, I could begin to see past the aging cabinets, mismatched tiles, and patched-in wood plank walls to reveal the bones of a sweet kitchenette. The adjoining petite dining nook was a welcomed bonus and gives this windowless kitchen natural light and some breathing room. A complete overhaul of the backsplash, floor tiles, lighting, cabinetry, and appliances in the kitchen is a done deal the

Room-Only Kitchen

day I scratch off that winning lottery ticket, but until then those looming limitations have motivated a slew of accessible and clever for-the-moment décor and storage ideas that I could do by myself right here, right now. These mini-improvements on a mini-budget will make a big impact in the functionality and livability of any pocket-sized kitchen, while keeping the design posh and portable. Grab a cup of coffee and give these *DTNT* ideas a whirl.

AFTER

51

Decorate and highlight architectural details even if they are faux real,

not

surrender to plain jane flat walls.

The problem with small spaces is that they're usually short on character-building architectural details. Adding the vertical scalloped faux molding helps to establish a visual separation between the living room and the dining nook, while still maintaining the overall flow of the entire living space, and it gives the eye an up-and-down path to follow on the walls, lifting the lid off an otherwise boxy room. Painting the molding with tonal shades of the base color creates a smooth transition from room to room without jarring the senses.

*miy*PROJECT

Measure and equally divide the wall into vertical sections. On these walls, ¾-inch-wide molding strips are installed 17 inches apart. Home improvement stores will gladly cut wood molding to size at no additional charge, and many offer self-serve cutting stations. Paint the molding strips and let dry. Attach to wall with a few small finishing nails. Next, flank wood molding with scalloped painter's tape running down the left and right side from ceiling to floor. Repeat for all wood molding strips. Paint inside the scallop-taped outlines with a companion paint shade found on the same paint chip card as the base wall color. Let dry, and peel off the tape to reveal a scallop design.

tip 👉 *When removed, the finishing nails leave very tiny holes behind that are easy to patch and paint. For a noncommittal option, removable adhesive strips can be used to install wood molding without wall damage.*

Decorate and conceal dingy ceramic floors under interlocking rubber tiles, *not* invest in pricey tile demolition.

When it came to tackling the faded tile floor in this cottage kitchen, a for-the-moment fix came to the rescue in the form of white rubber coin-flex tiles, commonly used on basement and garage floors. Industrial rubber tiles seemed fresh and a little unexpected dressing up a kitchen floor, and best of all, they fit the slim budget. The rubber flooring is easy to clean, clicks into place right over the existing tile floor without adhesives, and is cut to fit with a simple craft knife or scissors. If one rubber tile gets damaged or stained, it is a cinch to replace, and the entire flooring is removable at a moment's notice.

tip ☞ *Rubber flooring in the kitchen cushions the fall of wayward glasses and china, which tend to bounce instead of break upon impact. My favorite chip-free coffee cup is proof positive.*

Decorate with a tall counter-height table and chairs, *not* a standard dining set that shrinks the look of a nook.

It's always a wonder how much a few inches can make or break a space. In this very narrow dining alcove, choosing to use a counter-height table and chairs (about six inches taller than a standard dining set) gives the illusion of taking up less space than their shorter counterparts. Longer table legs expose more floor space, tricking the eye toward spacious, not skimpy. In this nook, guests also sit up closer to the window, taking full advantage of the light and view. Using more than two chairs with high backs looked and felt too hemmed in, but mixing in a few backless, metal industrial stools created a relaxed, airy flow in this crowded corner.

BEFORE

57

tip 👉 To combat the look of visual clutter and for added comfort, wood was added to the tops of metal stools to coordinate with the wooden French bistro chairs. Vintage brass hotel key tags were also glued to the backs of all the stools and chairs to unify the seating as an eclectic yet harmonious set.

tip 👉 If your eat-in alcove is long and narrow, opt out of using a standard kitchen table and consider a butcher-block counter on wheels instead. Readily available in much narrower widths, butcher-block tables come as skinny as 18 inches wide, compared to the average dining table, which starts at 30 inches wide on the petite side.

Decorate vertically and install a semi-handmade hanging pendant lamp,

settle for garden-variety recessed ceiling lights.

A dining nook, no matter how small, needs to have atmosphere, and this oversized, billowy white pendant lamp seems to float elegantly above the table as it draws the eye up and out. A little spray mount and embossed sheer fabric layered over the folds of the shade transforms this lamp from off-the-rack to custom atelier in a snap.

tips ☞ *For an organic textural twist, a sisal rope lamp cord tied in a figure-eight knot becomes an artful design accessory in the room.*

Pendant lamp converter kits are as easy to use as screwing in a light bulb. They transform any recessed light into a space-heightening pendant lamp.

Decorate and cloak windows with a frosted privacy layer, *not* impede precious light with shades or curtains.

It is a small-space design fundamental that natural light amplifies the perception of the size of a room. In this cottage, glorious sunlight comes streaming in from two small windows in the dining area, but the view of the shared courtyard below makes privacy an imperative. Café curtains looked too fussy for the space and kept getting caught behind dining room chairs, so a more compact design solution was needed. Designer-printed window film was overpriced for the job at hand and does not provide privacy at night when the interior lights are on. I learned this mistake quickly! Instead, good old-fashioned acrylic frosted glass paint (from a bottle, not from an aerosol spray can) and white chalk paint, along with a wall stencil, give these windows the maximum coverage they need, night and day, while costing 75 percent less than store-bought window film. The paint can be easily removed with window cleaner and a small razor blade to scrape off any stubborn spots.

*miy*PROJECT ☛

*miy*PROJECT

For foolproof camouflage on windows, brush one to two coats of frosted glass acrylic paint (again, from a bottle, not an aerosol spray) as a primer base coat and let dry. Use painter's tape to position the scallop stencil on top of the painted base coat and fill in the design with two layers of white chalk paint, depending on the desired level of coverage. This will give the window a sophisticated two-dimensional look.

Decorate and bring life and breath to a congested corner with air plants as hanging art,

not

overwhelm a snug spot with potted plants.

Adding a touch of nature to a wall has the potential of de-stressing claustro-phobic spaces without crowding the tabletops and floor with pots and plant stands. A simple MIY floating frame made from a sheet of clear acrylic, metal spacers, and 3½-inch screws allows the art print to protectively hang behind the frame with small magnets. Mist plants two to three times a week and give them a twenty-minute soak in water every other week. Remember to hang them in bright, indirect light.

tip ☞ *Your neighborhood hardware store will cut acrylic to size for free if you purchase from them.*

tip ☞ *Clear plastic tablecloth clips, available at any party supply outlet, gently cradle air plants onto the front of the frame to blend in as living art. Attach with clear, removable Command Brand poster strips.*

Decorate and double a
kitchen's visual square footage
with mirrored columns, *not* with dull, matte finishes.

With no direct windows or any architectural detail to write home about, this galley kitchen needed some transformative mirror magic to help expand the look of its lean footprint. The biggest style impact for the least amount of time and money was to add beveled, mirrored tiles, available at any home improvement store, to cover the entire height of two wall columns flanking the entrance to the kitchenette.

*miy*PROJECT

As luck would have it, mirrored tiles come in 12-by-12-inch squares, which fit the width of the column and would only require one custom cut on the bottom tile. Most hardware stores will make a simple straight cut on glass for little or no fee. Use mastic or mirror adhesive to attach mirrors to the wall, and use masking tape to keep tiles in place while they dry. The tiles have a tendency to shift while the adhesive dries.

tip ☞ *For a more flexible installation option, mirror-like acrylic wall decals come in a wide range of modern style options, and grouped together they add just the right amount of reflection and shimmer to make a tight spot sparkle. Best of all, they are removable without damage to walls.*

Decorate the inside of cabinets with removable fabric as revolving mini-canvases,

be stuck with prefab shelving.

Adding personality and a little drama to a postage-stamp-sized kitchen is as important as maximizing its storage potential. Lining the backs of open cabinets with fabric and liquid starch as the glue has a way of deflecting attention away from the scarcity of square inches in a space. Fabric easily peels off when you move or change your mind, without damage to cabinetry.

tip  *Buy and stock your pantry with water and wine glasses that stack on top of each other. Many chic styles on the market are not only available in plastic, but also in glass. Also, increase shelf space by an additional four to five inches by alternating the stems of wine and champagne glasses up and down.*

miy PROJECT

Use nonaerosol spray starch for best results, and saturate precut fabric (leaving one extra inch on all sides for shrinkage during drying) before applying on cabinets. Smooth out bubbles, spray two or more layers of starch, wipe off any excess and let dry. Trim excess fabric with a craft knife.

Decorate and amplify the proportions of a kitchenette with peel and stick marble vinyl on the backsplash, *not* be locked in to existing tacky tiles.

A kitchen backsplash is a natural focal point that can make or break a space, but if yours is more like a train wreck people gawk at for all the wrong reasons, peel and stick vinyl printed in faux marble is the ideal for-the-moment style cover-up. Installing the removable vinyl taller and wider than the shelving on the wall tricks the eye into believing the overall dimensions of the space are more generous than they really are.

*miy*PROJECT

Cut marble-printed contact paper into subway tile look-alike rectangles (3½ inches by 6 inches each for this backsplash) and affix to the existing tile or wall. Much like you would tile a wall, center the first adhesive *tile* and work your way out left and right horizontally. Leave a sliver of wall space between each tile to mimic the look of grout lines. Finally, frame the marble tile design with wood picture molding that will boost this look from faux to fab. Attach molding with removable adhesive wall strips for a noncommittal installation.

tips 👉 *Look for ways to hang a dish rack off the counter, which can be a game changer in a petite kitchen. Inexpensive dish racks are available with hooks that hold on to an existing shelf ledge or utensil rail.*

Rest narrow marble cheese boards on the edge of a slim kitchen sink to extend usable counter space.

Decorate with a mixed medley of cabinet hardware for added depth in a pint-sized kitchen,

conform to carbon copy fixtures.

A neutral space like this plain white kitchen benefits from the warmth and contrast that comes from the unexpected blending of metallic, crystal, and mercury glass cabinet hardware. To help stretch the kitchen décor budget, pricier mercury glass cabinet knobs dress up the larger, prominent cabinet doors; smaller and more affordable crystal knobs are the perfect fit for the lower cabinets; and industrial nickel drawer pulls are strong enough for the heavier drawers. The secret to keeping this petite kitchen from looking like a flea market lost-and-found is to choose a dominant metal, like nickel, to unify the look. The shiny mercury glass plays off the crystal and is grounded by the matte nickel drawer pulls for a cohesive, collected-over-time look and a winning personality.

tip ☛ *If your stainless-steel fridge is only stainless from the front, like mine is, adorn the sides with a practical metal magnetic board. Group several together to make one large magnetic message board. Glue super-strong magnets on the back to hold securely on to the fridge. Add hooks and storage caddies to help organize your nook.*

Decorate and swap out an old, light-obstructing kitchen door,

not

suffer cave-like conditions.

Don't underestimate an interior door as a strategic design feature in your petite nest. Although this windowless kitchenette runs straight into the master bedroom, a closed door would block the natural light flowing into this narrow niche. Swapping out the existing door for a salvaged secondhand find gave me the freedom to cut and modify it on a dime. Most landlords will remove and store the old door for you without a fee or complaint. By cutting out the top panel of this door and adding a prefab wood artist panel hinged in its place, light and air can flow between rooms while creating a decorative, whimsical Dutch door-like partition between the fridge and the bed next door. A collage of vintage, culinary tchotchkes, all painted in a matte white, is an artful, space-saving way to display a collection and clear out your drawers!

miy PROJECT ☞

Lightweight and affordable solid-wood painting panels, available in a variety of sizes at art supply stores, make for sturdy ad hoc Dutch doors. Custom-cut and install a mirror onto the reverse side of the wood frame so it adds sparkle and reflects the light into the bedroom as well.

Paint the panel and each kitchen object with white chalk paint and let dry. Arrange the collage and glue collectibles onto the front of the wood board. Think about mixing in the chemical equation for sugar in woodblock letters and numbers for fun. When dry, attach the wood panel with cabinet hinges to the door.

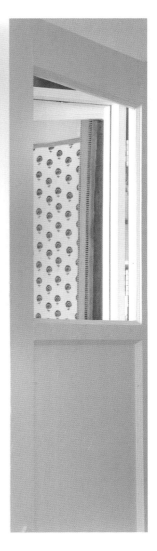

tip 👉 *For an easy-to-install closure, glue one small, round magnet to the bottom- and top-right corner of the opened (and unhinged) side of the wood panel. Let dry, then dab the front of the magnets with lipstick. Close the panel so it touches the doorframe. The lipstick marks exactly where to push in a flat-head metal thumbtack. Now the panel will stay securely closed when not in use.*

Decorate and maximize unused vertical nooks above stoves and refrigerators with storage-boosting baskets,

consume precious counter space.

Deep baskets hold pots and pans and party stemware (even my art supplies) over the stove, while baskets on top of the fridge keep a stockpile of paper towels and cookbooks in line, instead of squeezing them into crowded cabinets and spilling out over countertops. These baskets have traveled with me from one nutshell to the next, and I couldn't effortlessly negotiate my way around a cramped kitchen without them. An extra wooden shelf was installed over the stove, keeping storage baskets easily accessible.

p.s. *Renters, take heart! When it comes to installing clean white shelving in a kitchen, most landlords will welcome the addition with preapproval.*

tip ☞ *Most small-space dwellers have little choice but to store brooms and mops out in the open in their kitchen. To create an instant feeling of calm instead of chaos, spray-paint broom and mop handles a clean layer of white and hang on white hooks so they blend into the walls.*

tip ☞ *Double your usable prep area right over the stovetop by adding four wooden candle cups (about 1⅝ inches tall), found at any craft store, as "lifts" to the bottom of a cutting board. The cups have predrilled holes and are easily screwed into the cutting board. The new feet will raise the board high enough to stand securely over most stovetop burners.*

tip ☞ *Give lazy Susan trays a spin in a loaded kitchen corner. They look designer chic in marble and are ready to store or serve at a moment's notice while keeping everything within easy reach. My marble lazy Susan sits on the counter, keeping paintbrushes under control and in one place.*

Decorate and install sleek, sculptural storage solutions over the door,

not

crowd congested kitchen counters.

If you can't hide it, flaunt it. In a puny kitchen, don't overlook the spots above the door for untapped storage gold. The slatted wine holder keeps vino storage out in the open, and the arrangement of angled bottles gives this neglected alcove some architectural integrity and a space-heightening advantage.

tip ☞ *Give a thrift store ice bucket a new lease on life as an indoor planter. Wrap scalloped painter's tape halfway down and around the planter, and paint above the tape line to create a pattern. Remove tape while paint is still damp, and enjoy.*

tip ☞ *For added whimsy, tie a DRINK ME tag onto the wine rack, or hang it from one of the bottles.*

Decorate and upcycle humble kitchen tools into unexpected lighting,

not

spend a fortune on off-the-rac*k* lamps.

Call it *kitchen kitsch*, but vintage egg-beaters and large enamel colanders can inspire cool, one-of-a-kind lighting on a shoestring. Attach a colander and a flea market hand mixer with the help of a recessed light converter kit.

CHAPTER 3

Bitty but Bold

> "More is more and less is a bore!"
>
> —Iris Apfel, style icon, 2012

I remember when I lived in a junior one-bedroom apartment—one of those questionably legal, converted studios with a false wall, found a dime a dozen in New York City. The bedroom was just large enough to cram a full-size mattress into one corner, flush against the wall, leaving one foot of wiggle room on the left and half that much at the end of the bed. My in-laws came over to visit for the first time and innocently tossed their winter coats and scarves into the room, thinking it was the closet. I can laugh now, but it was embarrassing at the time. Needless to say, I have earned my stripes from the small-space decorating frontlines in my quest for storage and décor tips that make the most of a tiny footprint.

During those early years of trying to master the challenges of small-space living, it was pure instinct to pack as much as I could under the bed, hanging behind doors and up on the walls until the bedroom started to look and feel like a storage locker. I also felt the pressure to subscribe to a more restrained, muted color palette, with sleek white-on-white Scandinavian (aka Ikea) furnishings, which I assumed were the most efficient ways to maximize light and square inches in a pocket-sized bedroom, but that design approach never felt like me. Today, my true maximalist design tendencies are fully out of the closet. Layering an itty-bitty boudoir with sumptuous colors, bold patterns, soft fabrics, and cozy pillows is as vital to me as creating winning storage solutions.

Typical of most petite bedrooms, a shrunken floor plan is only one shortcoming in a long list of flaws to contend with. On the upside,

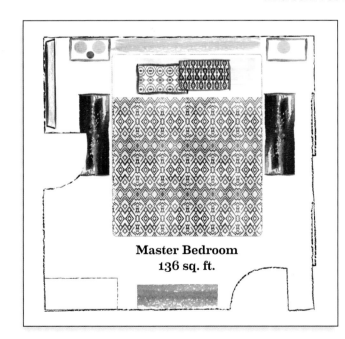

**Master Bedroom
136 sq. ft.**

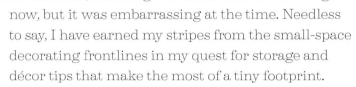

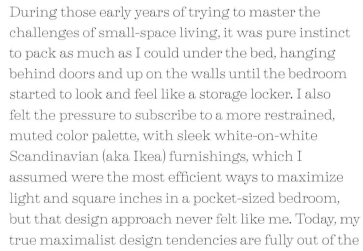

Bedrooms

Master Bedroom

BEFORE

AFTER

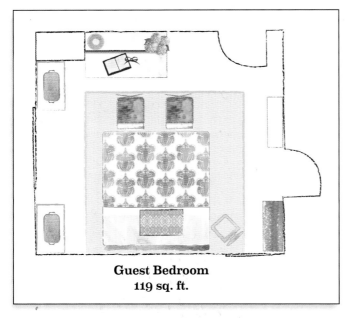

**Guest Bedroom
119 sq. ft.**

this cottage is blessed with two bedrooms, both with windows facing west for a pleasant stream of natural light for most of the day. But the thrill of having decent sun exposure starts to dim when you realize the 136-square-foot master bedroom opens straight into the kitchen. In five tiny steps from the bed, you're at the refrigerator. Keeping the bedroom door closed would only block the natural light flowing into the windowless kitchen. Next up on the list of fabulous flaws, the master bedroom shares a wall with an adjoining cottage, so some sound-buffering solution must land on the top of the fix-it list. And did I forget to mention the iron security bars that cover both bedroom windows, with a direct view into the next-door neighbor's house? Good times!

Now, on to the guest bedroom. Weighing in at a respectable 119 square feet, the guest bedroom must double as a craft and sewing supply room—housing an extensive fabric, paint, and paper collection, along with power tools—while providing out-of-town guests with a tranquil retreat. No easy feat.

Take a deep breath, and let's check off that fix-it list together one by one. Let's do this!

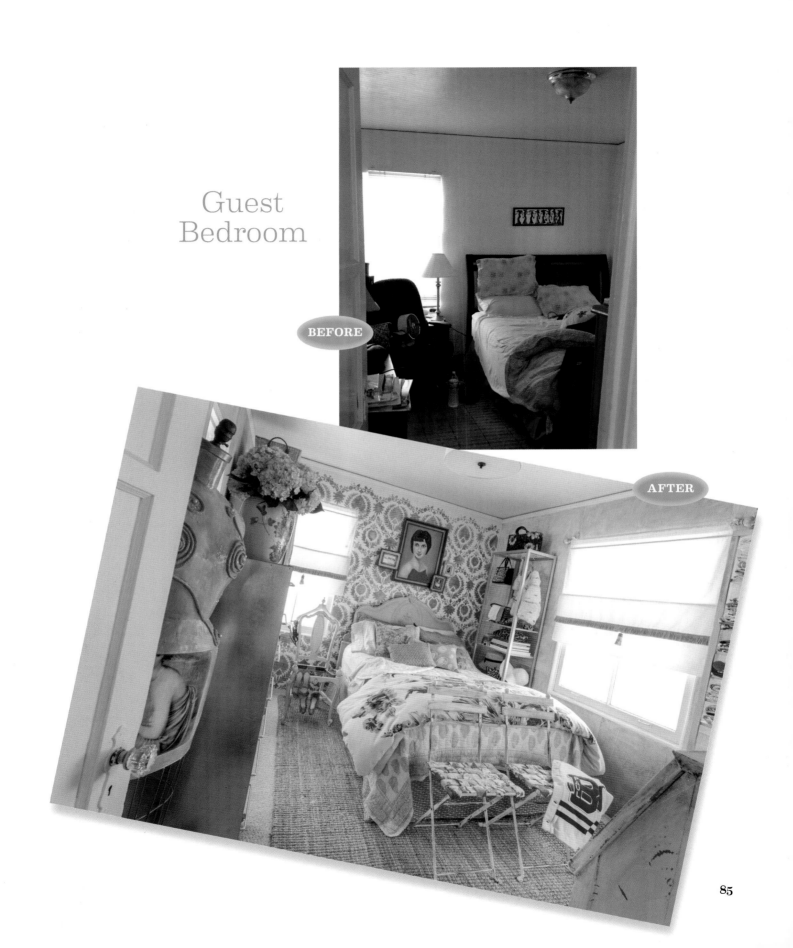

Guest Bedroom

BEFORE

AFTER

Decorate and paint a sun-deprived bedroom a soothing neutral, *not* **flat white.**

One of the biggest misconceptions about small-space design is that white walls make a bedroom appear more spacious, brighter, more relaxing, and less cluttered. Here's the problem: it takes a tremendous amount of natural light, from dawn to dusk, to make white walls come alive and not appear dull and sterile. This master bedroom is located very close to the building next door, and although it gets natural light throughout the day, it is filtered and shaded, making the former plain white walls look muddy. Instead, painting the room a relaxing, neutral gray-taupe makes the space feel and look expansive, not boxed in, and offers a neutral backdrop for splashes of color and pattern to come into play for an added dose of happy.

tips 👉 There are many neutral paint colors that work splendidly in small bedrooms. Look for soft taupe, pale blue, grays, greige, and creamy camel. Don't be afraid to ask your local paint shop to tweak paint shades to meet your needs. This bedroom is painted in Sherwin-Williams' Amazing Gray with only 70 percent saturation.

To mimic the look of wallpaper without the hefty price tag and messy installation, small white vinyl decals in the shape of stick trees were added to create an all-over pattern on the taupe-gray walls. The individual decals are removable, reusable, and fabulously frugal compared to the price of removable wallpaper, which would run into the hundreds of dollars to cover a small four-by-eight-foot wall. The trick is to use multiples of a small-scale wall decal design instead of large ones, which would lean more toward dorm room décor.

BEFORE

Decorate and drape the bed in one color family and go wild with prints, *not* **be tentative with pattern.**

In a junior-sized bedroom, a few luxurious layers on the bed can elevate the entire room from stark to cozy chic, without taking up extra inches. Choose one color, like blue, as the design anchor, then layer in two large-scale patterns. Next, mix in three or four smaller patterns in shades of the same color for a delightful contrast and added depth in a ho-hum sardine can of a space. Repeating the same colors from pattern to pattern will keep the design looking cohesive and intentional, not haphazard.

tip 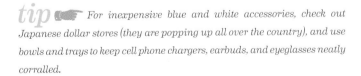 *For a quick, no-sew bed makeover, drape a plain queen-sized headboard with just two yards of fabric and some well-placed T-pins.*

tip ☞ *For inexpensive blue and white accessories, check out Japanese dollar stores (they are popping up all over the country), and use bowls and trays to keep cell phone chargers, earbuds, and eyeglasses neatly corralled.*

Decorate and layer the bedroom with a playful mix of masculine and feminine elements,

with one neutral comforter.

Decorative layers can also come in the form of gender-biased colors, fabrics, textures, and patterns, and blended together they impart a plain bed with warmth, sophistication, and balance. Choosing bed linens that mimic the pattern of a man's tailored shirt, paired with a boyish, baby-blue paisley quilt, plays in contrast with the unabashedly feminine floral duvet cover and pink-stenciled walls.

tip 🖝 *After layering your bed, step back, take a photo from different angles, and tweak. A photo allows you to see your space from a fresh, objective vantage point.*

Decorate and attach a no-sew bed skirt to a platform bed, **not** **reveal the secret stash underneath.**

Denizens of diminutive digs covet under-bed storage as if it were gold (I would be lost without it), and bed skirts help keep unsightly storage bins quietly under cover *unless* you have a platform bed. The sleeker profile of a platform bed is a top choice for small spaces, but the slatted-wood support beams that hold the mattress prevent a bed skirt from lying flat without damage to the fabric. Pre-hemmed table runners found at discount outlets carry a small price tag and are large enough to cover the longest side of a queen- or king-size bed without having to create a seam.

Decorate and feign the look of architecture with large-printed patterns on the wall, **be size-ist with a teensy-weensy bedroom.**

Small is not a mandate for decorating with tiny patterns and quiet colors. Going big and bold in strategic spots—with a dominant Suzani pattern in raspberry pink (Sherwin-Williams Cerise), for instance—enlivens a space with visual punch, alludes to a sense of architecture where none exists, draws the eye up, and pushes the walls out. Rather than inciting a bout of claustrophobia with four loud patterned walls, only the wall behind and directly across the bed is stenciled for a *bookend*, cocoon effect in the bedroom.

tip 👉 *If you are going to go BIG with patterns and colors, ground them with neutrals to give your eye a place to rest. The distressed gray French headboard, muslin window shades, and white secretary desk offer enough contrast for the raspberry pink to take center stage without being a scene-stealing diva. And don't forget relying on patina as a neutral too. Accessories and mirrors showing a little age, with peeling paint or a rusty metal finish, help to tone down a color-rich niche.*

*miy*PROJECT

Here's a low-risk way to bring in a pop of color: make it sheer! Mix your paint with a glazing medium (also called faux paint latex glaze) found at home improvement and craft stores. By adding one part paint to four parts glazing medium, the color becomes a little more sheer and translucent. The glaze does not change the hue or shade, just the saturation of the paint color.

Prime your walls with a base coat of white paint and let dry. Divide and tape off the wall equally into rectangles (these measure 24 inches wide by 31 inches tall). The same raspberry pink paint used on the stenciled walls is mixed with glaze medium and painted over the white base coat so the white peeks through. While it's still wet, drag a 17-inch wooden wire brush (available at dollar stores) horizontally across, picking up some of the paint as you go. Wipe off wire bristles, and repeat until you get to the bottom of the taped-off rectangle. Wipe off bristles again, and back at the top, drag the brush vertically all the way to the bottom, repeating until a stippled crisscross pattern covers the entire taped-off portion of the wall. Paint the glaze on every other rectangle, let dry, and then reposition painter's tape to the inside edge of the painted rectangle, creating a decorative seam in between the rectangles

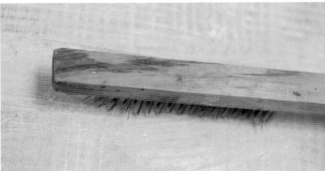

Decorate and bolster the bed with a headboard,

set the mattress bare against the wall.

A bedroom is not fully *dressed* without a headboard, but it is astonishing how many petite bedrooms I see that go without. There is a misnomer that a headboard takes up too much space in a compact bedroom. In fact, a taller headboard anchors the bedroom without adding to visual clutter, and it introduces a vertical element that can help enlarge the sense of space. Whether it's an ad hoc headboard fashioned from chalkboard paint on a wall, framed out wallpaper, or a thrift store find like this one, bought and repainted for sixty dollars, a headboard can be chic, cheap, and cheerful.

tip ☞ *Make guests feel welcome with a clip-on reading light. No need to hassle with installation or to hide lamp cords. Here the cord is part of the design.*

Decorate *up* and *out* with picture frame risers above the bed,

not

only with a seen-it-done-it framed mirror.

After the bed itself, the wall above the headboard is the most valuable design real estate in the bedroom. To give a random collection of portraits a story line and some prominence on the wall, picture frame risers made from inexpensive wheelbarrow hanger hooks (available at hardware stores) bring some of the art forward, creating a dimensional and layered art wall. Use anchor-less Wall-Dog screws to secure them to the wall.

tip ☞ *For poker-straight picture hanging, download a carpenter's level app onto your phone. It's free, and you'll always have it nearby.*

Decorate and embed sound buffers in a bedroom with a padded fabric screen,

 not

be a slave to earplugs and sound machines.

Mastering the art of living small, more often than not, involves sharing a common wall or courtyard with neighbors, or facing a public street or noisy back alley. Professional soundproofing is very expensive and not practical for most small-space dwellers, but adding upholstered furniture like a tall, padded fabric screen, along with heavier insulated thermal drapes on windows, can help to damper noise in a room. The basic idea is to reduce the number of hard surfaces that tend to ricochet noise vibrations in all directions.

And on a psychological level, these soft room additions will cloak you in a feeling of warmth and security. In this cottage, the master bedroom shares a common wall where the bed is located, and placing a paneled screen behind the bed—lined with a ½-inch-thick layer of sound-absorbing cork sheets—creates a stylish and cost-effective sound buffer that can travel with you.

*miy*PROJECT

This fabric screen is made from tossed-to-the-curb solid wood doors. One door is cut in half lengthwise thanks to my local hardware store and hinged to the panel on the far left and right so they serve as upholstered wings for the ultimate cocoon effect. Staple upholstery batting to the front panels, and glue ½-inch-thick cork slabs to cover the back of each panel. Cover the front with designer fabric and the back with budget-friendly burlap using a staple gun. To reduce vibrational contact between the screen and the noise coming from the cottage next door, the screen leans toward the headboard and away from the wall.

🕐🕐🕐💰💰💰

tip ☞ *Don't let a fabric screen or a mirrored wall prevent you from hanging artwork. Decorate the surface like you would a regular wall, and hang art with an over-the-door or repositionable adhesive hook. Here, a simple wood poster hanger frame highlights the painting without interfering with the lines or pattern of the screen.*

97

BEFORE

Decorate with slimmer-scale vintage furniture,

hefty contemporary pieces.

Historically, older homes built in the 1940s and 1950s measured less than 1,000 square feet, and furniture manufacturers catered to a more modest floor plan with smaller-scale pieces. In this petite guest bedroom, the multitasking vintage secretary desk, which combines storage and a work surface in one, is leaner and less deep (by almost five inches) than its modern counterparts. Another benefit to buying vintage: retro pieces are often crafted from solid wood, not cheap veneer or particleboard, and are built to last.

Decorate and bolster a bedside corner with a catchall valet chair,

not

throw clothes on the bed or let them pile up on coat hooks.

In a jam-packed bedroom, my battle cry is "combine and conquer." In a mere 12 square inches, this chic flea market chair with added wood finials conquers clutter as a compact valet station, holding ten pairs of heels (even flats), hats, scarves, handbags du jour, and a blazer. And with a click-on tray, the chair fulfills the need for a petite nightstand. Gentlemen have relied on valet chairs for years to keep them organized, but none catered to a woman's daily wardrobe needs—until now. Go, girl power!

*miy*PROJECT ☞

Remove the seat from a flea market chair (look for one that has a lower stretcher bar for added storage potential). Find a wide wood coat hanger and pull out the wire hook from the top of the hanger. Screw in a decorative wood finial in its place. Attach a wooden hanger to the chair back with two square bend screw hooks (#106). These hooks are L-shaped, with one end fitted with screw threads.

Drill two small pilot holes into the back of the chair, $\frac{1}{2}$ inch from the top. Each hole should be about one inch to the left and right of center on the chair back. Screw hooks into holes, leaving L-shaped ends pointing up. Next, rest the hanger on top of the L-shaped screws, and mark the underside where the second set of holes should be. Make sure the front of the hanger is facing toward the front of the chair. Drill the holes, fill with glue, and insert the L-shaped ends into the holes while glue is still wet and let dry. Paint the chair and hanger your favorite color to match the room's interior. Add dowel screws to the bottom of wood finials, and screw finials into the front corners of the chair and on the top left and right of the chair back. Then screw in craft balls to the front and back of the stretcher bars below to hold flats and loafers.

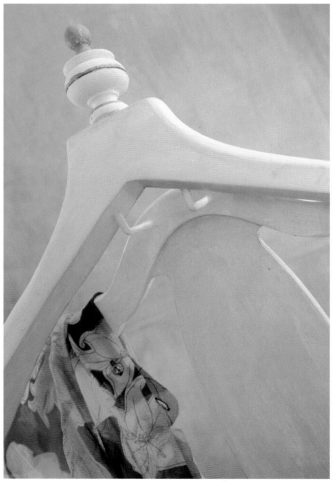

tip 👉 *A valet chair can moonlight as a nightstand with a clip-on tray! Simply glue two metal grip clips (available at any hardware store) and affix the flat side of the clip to the bottom of the tray, leaving the grip tongs open and free. Let dry, and clip the tray onto the chair seat frame closest to the bed to hold a cell phone, eyeglasses, or a bottle of water.*

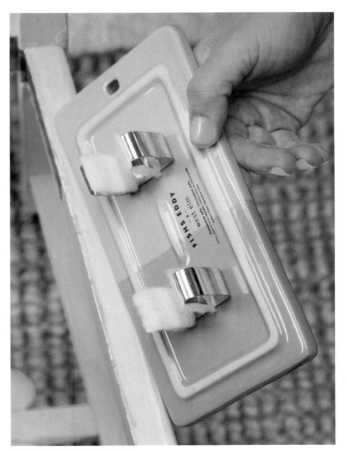

Decorate and embrace open shelving as a storage solution in a bedroom, cram clutter under the bed or in a closet.

At some point, every veteran small-space nester must surrender to the fact that not all clutter-free solutions in a bedroom can be hidden and tucked away. There is only a finite amount of closet and under-the-bed real estate available in teeny bedrooms. Bookshelves (preferably with no side panels, for that open, airy feel) are the dependable, go-to storage option, and with a coat of gold spray paint and a few ceiling hooks, a metal bookcase can appear more boudoir-chic than utilitarian-generic.

tip ☞ *Mix in display objects of varying heights, like these vintage trophies, to show off and stack hats and scarves.*

tip 👉 *To maximize the number of shoes you can fit on a shelf, organize shoes heel to toe on open shelving. This little shoe swap gives you a quick peek at color, toe style, and heel height and will help get you dressed and out the door in a jiff!*

Decorate and install vertical *miy* valet hooks,

rely on closet rods to organize a packed-to-the-brim wardrobe.

In this narrow master closet, there is only one closet rod to speak of, which barely holds a season's worth of clothing. There is not enough wall space to install a second rod along the opposite side, and piling clothing onto coat hooks never worked for me. It's important to see everything I have at a glance without creating a wrinkled wardrobe. This time around, inexpensive accordion bathroom mirrors (for less than the price of a movie ticket) are upcycled as MIY valet coat racks. Each accordion metal slat keeps hangers neatly in line, and because the racks swivel flat to the left and to the right, you have access to the back of the closet without breaking a sweat.

tip 👉 *To maximize space between accordion valet hooks and to keep clothing wrinkle-free and tidy, use junior-sized hangers that measure 14 inches across. Most clothes hangers measure 17 inches wide to cater to men and women of all sizes. These slimmer junior hangers fit unstructured women's jackets and blouses perfectly without overcrowding.*

*miy*PROJECT

Adding a wood craft ball in place of the mirror creates the perfect spot to hang a hat or two. Easily remove the mirror to reveal a flat-head screw. Next, drill a pilot hole in the bottom of a 2½-inch craft ball and attach the ball over the existing screw by twisting and turning it until the ball touches the bottom of the screw. Install each valet rack to the wall with anchor-less Wall-Dog screws to reduce wall damage, in case you need to take these racks with you.

Decorate with tall, skinny *kitchen* storage on wheels, *not* landlocked storage units.

Mobility on wheels eases the pressure of living in tight quarters. This chef's pantry cart effortlessly moves from the kitchen to the guest room, providing ample storage for craft supplies, and—as an added perk—the cart's tall and slim silhouette helps elongate the look of the bedroom. An MIY burlap cover keeps everything under wraps when guests come to town. And in the use-what-you-have spirit, a remnant vintage French grain sack from a previous project became the center of the design.

Decorate and conceal window security bars behind plantation look-alike shutters,

block the light like the room was a jail cell.

The master bedroom has two strikes against it: iron security bars that cover both windows, and a direct view into the house next door. Blinds and curtains got in the way of opening and closing the vintage double-hung windows and offered very little privacy control where it was needed most. Ideally, custom cut and installed plantation shutters would be the winning solution, but the total cost did not fit in the budget. Instead, modifying inexpensive decorative outdoor shutters, double-hung to look like plantation shutters, cost 60 percent less. Prefab solid wood shutters (avoid hollow MDF board shutters) fit the bottom half of the windows. The remaining shutters were cut in half and hinged to fit the upper half of the window. Most local neighborhood hardware stores will make a single straight cut in the wood shutters for a nominal fee.

tip ☞ *Leaning a large mirror against the wall not only adds reflection and vertically enhances the look of a bedroom, but it also provides a sneaky storage hideaway. In the master bedroom, there is enough coverage behind a jumbo mirror to tuck in a folding stepladder and a portable fan while still allowing for easy access.*

Decorate and maximize light and privacy on a dime with adjustable magnetized roman shades,

not

hard-to-install prefab blinds.

The guest room has big, bold patterns and colors on the walls and layered on the bed, so window treatments needed to be simple and sleek. Affordable, prefab roman shades from a big box store are made with magnets and metals rods in the seam, so they easily adjust up and down without strings or pulleys. They attach to the wall with two small cup hooks. Add sisal trim fringe and a tassel for a custom finish.

*miy*PROJECT ☞

Atelier finishes like fabric trim or a champagne cork tassel pull personalize and soften the edges of a stark bedroom without appearing as clutter. Use a small eyelet screw found at any hardware store and insert into the top of a champagne cork. Use your home printer to make an 8½-by-11-inch copy of a vintage print, favorite poem, or handwritten letter. Printing on off-white parchment paper gives the tassels a vintage look. Fold the paper in half lengthwise twice so it measures 8½ inches by 2¾ inches. Next, fold the paper in half in the opposite direction so it measures 4¼ inches by 2¾ inches.

While still folded, cut into the paper to create the tassel fringe, leaving a ¼-inch margin free of any cuts at the top of the paper. Wrap the fringed paper around a champagne cork, with the uncut folded side up at the top of the cork. Hold with your thumb and wrap the top with a ribbon. Secure the ribbon and the paper with a small gold thumbtack. Finally, thread the ribbon through an eyelet screw on top of the cork.

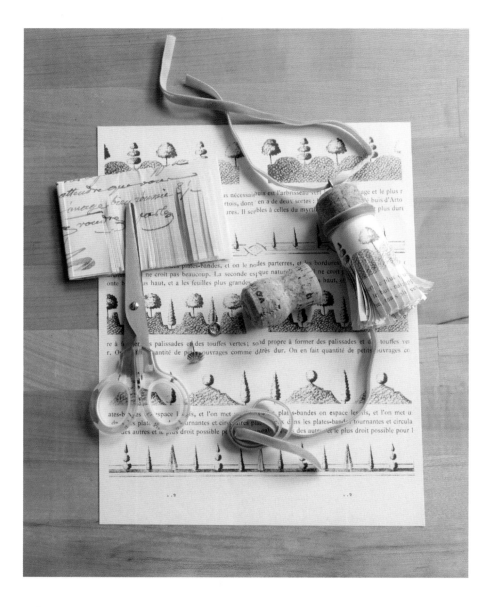

tip ☞ To camouflage the iron security bars on the windows and the street traffic from the front yard, paint the lower windowpanes with a very thin layer of frosted glass paint.

Decorate and layer a wall with a collection of small mirrors in the same finish, *not* limit reflection from one solo mirror.

In much the same way as a large mirror will magnify the look of a small space with reflective light and glow, a collection of smaller mirrors displayed as a group on a wall, united in the same frame or finish, acts as one large decorative window with a bit more design interest. Layer mirrors, like these made from vintage tart and pie pans with added craft mirrors, to create an eye-catching, radiant wall sculpture. When arranging a small collection of mirrors, decorate in odd numbers. The odd number grouping of objects is more appealing to the eye. Think three, five, seven, or more.

tip ☞ *For tiny tins, decoupage a laser print (inkjet prints will become too runny when wet with glue) of your favorite photo using Mod Podge glue under a piece of glass. Let dry, and glue upright onto the inside of a tart tin.*

Decorate and adorn
nightstands with an eclectic
pair of lamps, abide by must-match
decorating rules.

Flea market finds collected over the years can impart a feeling of intimacy and depth in a sparse bedroom. Keeping an odd pairing of lamps looking more cohesive and less chaotic depends on similar brass finishes, matching nightstands, coordinating shades, and equalizing their height. Lifting the shorter fox lamp onto a stack of books covered in handmade gold paper gives it enough decorative weight to appear as part of a balanced pair while still being quirky and unexpected.

tip ☞ *For added luminance, line the inside of a lampshade with gold paint or paper. The gold metallic sheen will counterbalance the unflattering glow of a compact fluorescent light bulb.*

Decorate and widen the look of a cramped bedroom with leggy, open-back nightstands,

clunky, solid tables that sit squarely on the floor.

Adorning the bed with a pair of nightstands, sitting up high on legs and offering a backless open shelf, makes a packed bedroom appear more spacious and airy. By allowing the eye to gaze all the way to the back wall instead of stopping short at the front, the open-back design eases that cooped-up feeling.

Decorate and extend the lounge zone with a pair of folding bistro chairs,

not

a bulky bench or ottoman.

Carving out a little sitting nook to read from at the base of the bed only takes a pair of folding bistro chairs, which helps to make a bedroom feel and function as more spacious and less restricted. Bistro chairs, with their lean profile, can easily slip into clipped corners and are more versatile than large ottomans or benches. When friends come to visit, the chairs team up as a sturdy luggage rack (that doesn't show dirt), or in a pinch they separate as additional guest seating inside or out into the garden for impromptu parties. For added comfort and style points, the chair seats are padded with a weave of thick upholstery fabric strips.

tip ☞ *Add simple craft ball finials to the top of the café chair for a handy place to hang a hat or bag.*

*miy*PROJECT

First, measure and cut upholstery fabric into strips to cover the wooden slats horizontally. Allow an extra 2½ inches of length on each side to tuck under the chair and double the thickness of the width of each strip. Fold the fabric strip in half lengthwise, centering the raw edge underneath. Use a staple gun to secure the strips to the bottom of the chair seat. A few additional staples are needed on the top of the seat to keep the webbing nice and secure. These staples will be hidden underneath the next layer of fabric weaving.

Next, measure and cut fabric strips to be woven vertically over and under the horizontal slats. Leave 2½ inches of length on each side, and double the thickness of each strip. Secure raw edges under the chair seat with a staple gun

tip 👉 *Seasoned small-space veterans know to tuck away a few guest chairs for emergencies, and here's a way to store them and make them work for you on their off hours. Hang a folding chair fully opened from the back door of a closet using over-the-door temporary hooks. Use the chair's frame to hang clothing and handbags and the seat to hold folded sweaters.*

Decorate and streamline an old dresser with recessed knobs for a slimmer silhouette, *not* use protruding hardware.

When every inch counts, knobs that stick out even half an inch from a dresser can be true barriers in a cramped bedroom. There has been many a sweater snagged and many a knee bruised negotiating my way through a narrow bedroom path. It's time for a hardware intervention. Old clunky hardware was swapped out for faux recessed bronze cabinet pulls that sit nicely flush in an old dresser without the difficulty of having to drill and fit a true recessed knob. It's a clever way to brighten up a rather drab piece and bring it into this decade.

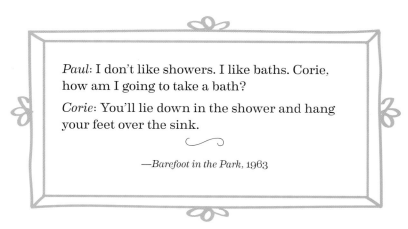

CHAPTER ·4· Jewel Box

Paul: I don't like showers. I like baths. Corie, how am I going to take a bath?

Corie: You'll lie down in the shower and hang your feet over the sink.

—*Barefoot in the Park*, 1963

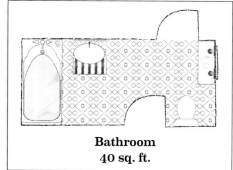

**Bathroom
40 sq. ft.**

From any vantage point this 1940s Jack and Jill bathroom, a quaint term for a shared powder room that opens up to two bedrooms, was average in every way: A standard-issue white pedestal sink—check! A big box store medicine cabinet—check! The ubiquitous beige crackle tile shower and floor—check, check! The bathroom also meets the US average for size, measuring an unremarkable 40 square feet, room for just the basics and not much more. The one asset is a medium-sized window that lets sun and fresh air flow in freely—ideal except for an unobstructed view into the next-door neighbor's bedroom. Maximizing the good over the bad and striving for *unique* over *mediocre* fuel my small-space living mantra, and it was about to be put to the test here.

The goal was to create a jewel box of a space, full of character and personality, with chic and mobile storage solutions that would be easy to install myself and affordable enough not to alarm my accountant. Because the bathroom opens up to both bedrooms, the overall design had to pop but still be cohesive with the surrounding spaces. My inspiration came from the chocolate-brown-and-white stripes of New York City's iconic store Henri Bendel. Vertical striping has a way of making a tiny space stand a little taller, and well, brown matches everything. I did a quick inventory of what I already had in my design storage closet that could be repurposed in this bathroom. Sophisticated brown shantung silk curtain panels, extra long, left over from my New York City bedroom would add volume and coverage to the stark window. And fresh from my former living room, a large collection of flea market picture frames, repainted in glossy white, would embellish the walls with architectural dimension without putting a dent in my credit card.

Bathroom

Now that I had a place to start, I was on a singular mission, researching and experimenting with the best products and materials that would offer design flexibility with one-of-a-kind style. I hope you'll be inspired by the clever ways I found to revive an ugly tile floor, soften hard vanity lighting, and double the storage potential of a run-of-the-mill bathroom without permanently altering the space. And remember that pesky privacy issue with the neighbors? Problem solved! It took some trial and error, but now I can look through both Jack and Jill entrances and see that the bathroom has evolved into the crown jewel of the cottage.

BEFORE

AFTER

123

Decorate and paint height-alluding vertical stripes in a petite powder room,

be resigned to hospital-white walls.

With a style nod to a beloved, iconic New York department store, chocolate-brown-and-white stripes transform this garden-variety cramped bathroom into a jewel box of a space. Vertical stripes have a magical way of creating a visual movement with the suggestion of more room from floor to ceiling. Go glossy on the paint finish for added reflective shine in the space.

tip 👉 *For a paint alternative, try using removable, vinyl decal stripes that are easily applied and will guarantee poker-straight lines without hurting walls.*

Decorate and amplify the look of a standard medicine cabinet mirror with custom magnetic frames, *not* **minimize a bathroom's greatest asset.**

It's simple decorating logic. The bigger the mirror, the bigger the bathroom appears to be. A wood frame embellished with craft wood pieces gives a plain vanity mirror more gravitas and presence. It attaches with magnets to a metal-framed medicine cabinet mirror for a noncommittal décor boost

*miy*PROJECT

Click together inexpensive wood artist stretcher bars, available in a variety of size combinations, to form a custom-fit frame for a generic vanity mirror. Glue on craft wood pieces in circle and teardrop shapes to form a relief design on the front. Paint. On the back of the frame, glue strong magnets to the corners and along the sides. The frame is lightweight and will stay secure every time you open the cabinet to grab your toothbrush.

126

Decorate and tuck in clutter-wrangling corner laundry baskets under a pedestal sink,

waste underutilized storage space below.

Slim pedestal sinks are often the default choice for a petite powder room, and while they don't take up much floor space, they offer zero hidden storage relief. A clever clutter-busting trick is to slip two collapsible corner laundry baskets—one for your lights and the other for your darks—under the basin as a winning space saver.

tip 🖝 *A wooden salad bowl swaps from the kitchen to hold soaps and guest towels in the powder room.*

Decorate and squeeze in a narrow sink shelf, **not** become a victim of a countertop recession.

With very little counter space to speak of, a clear glass shelf shimmies into the narrow backsplash, supported by a pair of lightweight polyurethane corbels. The corbels attach to the wall securely with Command Brand removable adhesive strips.

Decorate and step up your storage game with a teak bath caddy, **not** overload the hanging shower rack.

Whether you prefer to take a shower or enjoy deep soaks in the tub, rest an expandable bath caddy across the end of the tub full time for that extra space-saving shelf we all need. Stack hand towels along with your overstock of shampoo and body scrubs, leaving bathroom cabinets free and clear.

tip ☛ *Who says you can't hang art on a shower wall? Camouflage ugly tiles with a waterproof poster print. Laminate your favorite printed art at your local office supply shop, and display it in a glass-free acrylic frame. Attach to the tile wall with suction cups or repositionable clear hooks.*

tip ☛ *Add plastic baby-changing table hooks to hang loofah sponges and a back brush.*

Decorate and spotlight a humble guest towel hook for architectural rococo relief on a plain wall,

not

leave it hanging solo.

An ornate picture frame (without the backing or glass) feigns the look of architectural molding, which adds dimension to an otherwise bland bathroom. A high-gloss paint finish reflects the light and makes the frame pop from the wall. Now a hardworking towel hook garners the respect it deserves.

tip 👉 *A salvaged picture frame collection (relocated from my living room wall in NYC) gets a new lease on life prettying up a powder room.*

Decorate and soften harsh vanity lighting with a *not* expose wrinkles before their time!

Inheriting bad lighting, especially unforgiving downlights over a vanity, often comes with the *living-in-a-shoebox* territory. One quick, electrician-free trick is to modify a thrift store lampshade to bounce the light toward the ceiling, allowing a gentle cascade of diffuse light to illuminate the vanity and to reflect your most flattering self!

*miy*PROJECT

Remove all fabric from a secondhand lampshade frame. Measure and cut vellum paper (found at an office supply store) to fit all side and bottom panels, leaving the top and side facing the wall open and uncovered. With an all-over-the-page decorative hole punch (like this butterfly pattern), create a cutout design to allow for a little light to peek through. Press the hole punch halfway down into the paper to cut the outline of the wings while leaving the rest of the butterfly intact. Fold wings up and out. Glue paper panels to the sides and bottom of the shade. Attach a standard clip-on bulb adaptor that screws into the top of the lampshade and grips on to the light bulb. Use a nut to secure the screw to the top of the shade.

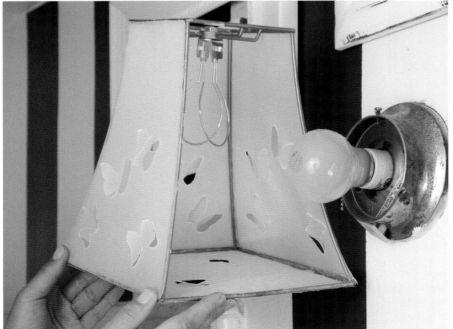

Decorate and install a train towel rack,

be limited to over-the-door storage solutions.

A train towel rack is at the top of my small-space survival list for bathroom storage and stands as a rare exception to the *Decorate This, Not That!* rule of portability. The rack holds an entire collection of bulky bath towels, frees up closet and shelf space without taking up an inch of real estate, and is affordable enough to leave behind and *pay it forward* to the next tenant. I've installed one in each rental apartment without objection from the landlord.

tip ☞ *For inexpensive towel racks, shop in the kitchen section. Sturdy stainless-steel dish rack shelving comes in a variety of sizes and is gently priced.*

Decorate and create a bonus layer of privacy with an enhanced adjustable window screen,

accidentally end up on YouTube.

Privacy literally goes out the window when frosted double-paned windows open up for some fresh air. But with a little spray adhesive and a stiff panel curtain from Ikea, an adjustable window screen keeps the air circulating with a little extra camouflage.

*miy*PROJECT

Choose a curtain panel made from a stiff polyester, and cut to fit the front and back of each screen panel. Use a layer of spray adhesive on each panel, and cover with the cut fabric pieces. Regular craft glue will leave visible marks on the screen when sun shines through it, so stay with a clear spray adhesive for the best results.

tip ☞ *Keep an eye out for bathroom storage boxes with magnetized sides. Now hairpins and tweezers have a convenient place to land.*

Decorate and broaden the look of a dingy floor with adhesive decals,

not

wait until the cows come home to retile.

If the only time your bathroom floor looks decent is when it's covered up by a wet towel, it's time for a quick sprucing up with removable and water-resistant floor tile decals that come in a large variety of styles and sizes (and can also be custom-cut per order). A larger-format Moroccan-inspired pattern teases the eye into believing this shrunken bathroom is larger than its four walls. (Floor tile decals by Bleucoin at Etsy.com.)

tip ☞ *Leave tile grout lines visible between decals to enhance the illusion of the real thing. Also, use white caulking to fill out and secure cut seams around the sink base and the toilet. It will keep water from seeping in underneath the decals and plays up the authentic tile look.*

Decorate and layer a petite powder room with scented soap bubbles, *not* toxic sprays and plug-ins.

Scent is the final décor layer to any space, and the right fragrance can truly elevate a teeny bathroom. Make your own scented bubbles and keep them out for guests to enjoy. It's an interactive, amusing way to keep your room smelling fresh and welcoming.

*miy*PROJECT

In a bowl, add fifteen to twenty drops of your favorite essential oil combinations, like lavender, pear, mint, or grapefruit, to ½ cup of unscented dish soap, available at health food stores. Next, add one tablespoon of glycerin (also found at health food stores), which will make the bubbles last longer. Finally, slowly pour in ¾ cup of distilled water. Stir gently to avoid agitating the bubbles. Decant the scented bubble mix into empty soap bubble bottles, and leave a sign that asks guests to blow a bubble or two.

Decorate and go vertical with hanging orchid moss balls for a counter-free touch of nature, *not* give in to souless, sterile tile walls.

Think of your bathroom as a petite greenhouse with microclimate conditions ideal for orchids and bromeliads to thrive and beautify. If there is not an inch of counter to spare for a potted plant, wrap your orchid in the kokedama moss ball technique and hang in bright, indirect light.

*miy*PROJECT

Remove the orchid from its pot, brush off any remaining soil, and set aside. Fill a nylon knee-high stocking with orchid bark and potting mix so it forms a firm ball that the orchid can sit comfortably on top of. Tie off the stocking top into a knot and cut the excess nylon off. Using clear nylon fishing line, secure orchid roots around the ball of orchid mix. Without hurting the roots, wrap several times until secure. Cover the ball with preserved moss and continue wrapping the moss in place with the nylon fishing line. Dip the entire ball in water and let drip dry in the sink. Hang your new orchid ball with a piece of twine made into a simple sling and insert two T-pins on each side of the twine into the moss ball for extra security. Mist with water once a week, and soak in water twice a month, depending on the humidity. Hang in bright, indirect light.

139

Pocket Gardens,

Brontë: And don't go in the greenhouse any-
more. That's all I ask.It's my special place.

Georges: Oh, you like your plants better than
people.

Brontë: Some people.

—*Green Card*, 1990

Society maven, best-dressed list
perennial, and celebrated horticulturalist C. Z.
Guest believed, "Having a garden is like having
a good and loyal friend." Until I moved into this
beach bungalow, I was never lucky enough
in my big-city life to have a garden patch,
balcony, or stoop that beckoned a meaningful
plant-to-human relationship. Too many indoor
potted casualties seemed to seal my fate as an
admirer of gardens from afar. But it all seemed to defy the laws
of genetics, since my parents have two green thumbs apiece and
can take a fruit seed or plant clipping and turn it effortlessly into
a blooming orchard. My mother speaks the same language
as flowers, especially roses, so with her encouragement and
her willingness to interpret, I ventured to revitalize this
small, dried-up plot in the only way I knew how—decorate
it like it was just another room. The same posh and portable
approach to small-space interior design was going to guide
me through to the great outdoors. But where to begin?

For decades this garden suffered the perfect storm of
neglect: a prolonged California drought, careless tenants,
and only spotty maintenance from an aging gardener who
should have retired long ago. The front lawn was no more;
only the weeds were winning. Remarkably, one loquat fruit
tree defied the odds and remained standing, and it gave
me hope. The future of this garden depended on drought-
resistant shrubs, low-maintenance flowers, and amending the
dense clay soil with mulch and compost. I was in way over my head

Terrace, Stoops

until I decided my emphasis would be on garden décor, not landscaping.

Just like the inside of the cottage, this petite and sparse yard, surrounded by a flimsy, distressed picket fence, needed key design features to anchor, elevate, and frame the space. A new, tall wood trellis with climbing sweet potato vines and a vintage bicycle turned flower planter established distinct zones in the garden and gave me the confidence to tread onward. Instead of lots of little plant clusters, a few larger pots along with whimsical architectural ornaments helped border plant beds and appear more like sculpture than clutter. And creating curved lines with used bricks gave this outdoor room a sense of discovery without breaking the budget. Finally, this featureless garden was starting to develop a personality with genuine curb appeal, but it is still a work in progress.

Full disclaimer: Transforming this garden in no way makes me a horticultural expert. The few plants I do feature in projects here were chosen because they are least likely to be fussy and die. What I do know is that layering your tiny terrace or petite garden patch with some of these unique space-maximizing décor tips and projects, flexible enough to take with you to your next abode, will expand the way you use your outdoor room and will give you the confidence to make it truly your own. And maybe, in the process, you will be like me and happily come to regard plants as friends.

BEFORE

AFTER

Decorate and frame a small yard
with a tall arbor,

deny visitors the pleasure of
making an entrance.

This garden looked shrunken when
bordered by a small wooden gate and a
short, faded fence. There was nothing
to give it any prominence or separation
from the street. A simple wood arbor
added to this old fence now creates
a more formal visual barrier while
framing a view into the garden. For
added portability, a smaller trellis on
wheels for each side of the fence can
have the same effect. Add climbing
vines in pots on either side for an
entrance that can travel with you.

Decorate and anchor an itty-bitty courtyard with a whimsical feature like a vintage bicycle built for flowers, *not* with just garden-variety pots and planters.

Beyond a drought-stricken tree in the front yard, there were no design focal points in this petite garden patch. Armed with the element of surprise and a brown thumb, I used an old garage sale bike, outfitted with a French metal basket and a cart of flowers, to set the playful tone for the rest of the yard and help distract attention from its diminutive dimensions.

tip ☞ *Upgrade and swap out the seat for a vintage Schwinn.*

tip ☞ *Any basket can become a bike basket. Use a pair of thrift store leather belts to attach the basket to the front of the bike.*

Decorate and add curves to a sparse yard with portable tree brick ring landscaping, *not* be confined by the straight lines you see in a parking lot.

Mixing curves with straight lines in a compact garden invites the eye to travel and creates an air of discovery. Simply stack used bricks (found free locally online) on top of a plastic weed barrier sheet. No mortar is needed. I opted out of using leveling sand to secure bricks in place, for fear of disrupting future planting in the area. When you move, disassembling the tree ring is easy, and people will gladly pickup the brick remnants.

tips ☞ *Don't be dissuaded by old mortar stuck on cast-off bricks. With a light tap of a hammer and a chisel, the mortar easily chips off.*

For a perfect circle, tie a string around a stick and place it in the ground where you want the center of the tree ring to be. Cut the string according to how large you want the circle to be, and tie the loose end of the string around a nail or a pencil. Pull and guide the nail around the dirt to imprint a complete circle as your guide.

Decorate, layer, and accessorize outdoor furniture like you would indoors, *not* concede to minimalist garden design doctrine.

A confined outdoor space reaches its maximum potential when it transitions easily as an extension of an indoor room with all the creature comforts. Accessorize your slice of nature with comfy pillows, throws, and candles.

tip ☞ *Don't shy away from bright, vivid colors outdoors. These Kelly green chairs are a standout and draw the eye into the garden patch.*

Decorate and squeeze in a wine table for two, **not** shy away from entertaining alfresco on a narrow balcony.

Any sliver of an outdoor space is a gift waiting to be shared. By outfitting a portable bamboo wineglass holder with wood wiggle molding (found in the back of hardware stores), the table balances nicely on the arms of two chairs, without crowding in on precious square inches elsewhere.

*miy*PROJECT

Turn the wine table over and measure ½ inch from the left and right sides of the table toward the center. Cut two pieces of wood wiggle molding to fit the length of the table. Glue or use screws to attach the two wood strips.

Decorate and stash garden
tools stylishly away in a
tricked-out basket,

not

scramble for a spade.

Even a small container garden on
a stoop requires a roundup of basic
tools, gloves, and a watering can, but
the average storage caddy is more
practical than pretty and tends to be
on the hefty side. Attaching pot rack
hanging hooks to the inside weave of
a slim, tall basket keeps gloves and
sheers organized, easy to see and
grab without monopolizing too much
deck space.

*miy*PROJECT

Top the basket off with a galvanized condiment holder filled with low-maintenance ivy so it can multitask as a planter. If the metal holder is a little too small for the basket opening, try wrapping the outer top side with a band of cork masking tape or sisal twine for a snugger, organic-looking fit. A dollar store plant dolly on the bottom of the basket, secured with plastic cable ties, keeps it mobile.

Decorate and border a thin garden bed with sculptural orbs, **presume they are reserved for stately manors only.**

Architectural garden ornaments can look right at home on small balconies or in modest green patches. In this garden, where there are thinning spots, these cement orbs contrast with the organic shapes of the plants, add an industrial touch, and keep weeds at bay.

miy PROJECT

Use a cement product like ShapeCrete, which can be molded, sculpted, and shaped like clay with the durability of cement. Mix with a little water and roll out a workable layer of clay. Drape over an inflatable beach ball as an armature. Leave a small opening on the bottom so the ball will sit flat on the ground. This opening will also allow you to deflate the beach ball once the cement is dry. Cement dries in about 48 hours and is outdoor-worthy in a week.

Decorate and pump up your curb appeal with a staghorn fern address plaque,

not

be limited to a by-the-numbers house sign.

Mounted on a taupe-gray chalkboard painted plaque, staghorn ferns command attention outside any petite home. Choose a partially shady spot with filtered light like a covered porch for your fern to thrive. Lay a bed of preserved moss on a wood board a little larger than the plant base, and screw in small stainless-steel screws around the perimeter of the fern. Remove soil from the fern roots and lay down on the moss base. Cover root ball with another sheet of moss, and secure by weaving fishing line in a crisscross across the fern.

Decorate and bolster an archway with tall urns that echo the design heft of stately columns,

be a shrinking violet with your garden entrance.

A modest wood arbor seems to stand a little taller boosted by two heavy urns, which are adorned with freshly cut flowers, giving a small garden a grander entrance.

tip ☞ *Clear cable ties at the base keep vases securely attached to the fence.*

Decorate and use an indoor pewter table outdoors, *not* worry about rust or tarnishing.

Because pewter does not generally contain iron, it will not rust, corrode, or tarnish outdoors. My old living room end table has a newfound purpose in the garden holding candles and cocktails, and the indoor-outdoor flexibility allows me to live a little larger in my tiny digs.

Decorate and delight guests with a living moss welcome mat, *not* underwhelm them with a dime-a-dozen rubber pad.

I am simply mad for moss. I love their texture and varying shades of green. If you have a shaded entrance (maybe a side or back door) that is not subjected to high foot traffic, then this project will elevate your humble porch instantly. Pillow and rock cap moss are durable and work best for this welcome mat design.

*miy*PROJECT

Purchase a rubber mat with a prefab cutout design, and cut a piece of cork to fit underneath the entire mat. Glue the bottom of the rubber mat to the cork base using contact cement. The glue will take a few days to cure properly. When dry, add a little spring water (not tap) into each cubby and press moss into place. Some moss pieces will need to be shaped to fit, using your fingers. Spray the entire moss mat with water when done and place on your doorstep. Mist with water every few days. Never let the moss dry out, but don't drench it.

Decorate and disguise an ugly porch with a custom-cut outdoor rug, *not* rely on a welcome mat to do the job alone.

Some say a porch is like the smile on the face of a house. If that's the case, then my porch is missing a few teeth and needs Botox. Unable to paint or resurface the porch with tile, an outdoor rug turned out to be the ideal portable solution. It is easy to cut and customize to the shape of your porch with scissors, and any raw edges can be folded over and secured with a string of hot glue. The outdoor rug rinses off with a hose, is mildew resistant, and the green and white stripes bring vitality to a dark porch.

Decorate and be playful with your outdoor décor,

cave into haughty horticultural design expectations.

A small terrace or itty-bitty backyard that may be short on acreage can go big with a sense of humor. Whimsical planters accessorize the porch and feel welcoming. Design for you, not your neighbors.

Decorate and illuminate a tiny garden with *miy* folding picture frame lanterns,

overstock on bulky candle holders.

Candlelight is the great equalizer. Everyone and everything looks more radiant basking in it, but outdoor lanterns take up a lot of space. If you have to store them during bouts of inclement weather, then your sweet little abode just got smaller. Instead, if you attach two wooden, double-hinged picture frames to create one square lantern, it can fold down flat and store away without taking up too many spare inches.

*miy*PROJECT

Remove the picture frame cardboard backing from two double-hinged picture frames. Glue the glass to the inside of each frame. Unfold both sets of frames so the front sides of the frame are facing each other. Screw in hinges on both unattached sides of the frames. Attach a bamboo purse handle (available at craft stores) to the top of the newly framed lantern. Place a flameless candle on a square plate and cover with the lantern.

Decorate and hydrate a petite container garden with chic self-watering stakes,

risk plants going bone dry.

Flower boxes and planters can transform any outdoor patch into a garden oasis, but containers dry out quickly in warmer months. Self-watering bottles can keep your plants moist and merry for almost a week, but most are short on style or are a little fragile. Instead of expensive and breakable glass watering globes, simply attach a 12-ounce plastic pomegranate juice bottle (love the shape of these), filled with water, onto a terra-cotta watering stake. Turn the bottle upside down and place in a pre-watered planter next to the root system. As your plants absorb more moisture from the soil, the stakes will automatically release water near the roots as needed. There is no danger of overwatering.

tip ☞ *To remove the bottle label, use fine steel wool and warm soapy water. Gently rub off printed label under warm water. The label will come off easily without leaving scratches on the plastic.*

Decorate and give a tiny plot gravitas with a large, stackable planter,

dwarf the garden with small plant clusters.

A few generously sized planters placed strategically around the yard can hide the limited boundaries of the garden, making it appear larger. Here a double planter also becomes a focal point for a modest porch. Try using two metal hanging baskets (these are 18 inches wide), and invert one as the standing base. Stack the other one on top so the bottom of the baskets meet, and secure with plastic cable ties.

tip ☞ *Just as you would with the interior décor, add texture and contrast outdoors with unexpected plant duos like a tropical bromeliad and classic English ivy. As long as the light and water requirements are compatible, this is a match made in heaven.*

CHAPTER 6

Entertain This,

"Have you heard?
It's in the stars
Next July we collide with Mars
Well, did you evah?
What a swell party, a swell party
A swellegant, elegant party this is!"

—Cole Porter, "Well Did You Evah?"

When it comes to throwing a grand party in a skimpy nutshell of a space, I'm a champagne glass half-full, not half-empty kind of girl. A lack of real estate never stopped me from celebrating occasions big or small in my humble abode. I've hosted swell parties for my nearest and dearest in spaces no larger than 300 square feet. Deciding to keep a Murphy bed pulled down in the middle of a narrow studio became the main attraction at a *Mad Men* cocktail hour and was a bona fide smash. At another event, it was BYOC—*Bring Your Own Chair*—a theme that turned out to be one of the evening's amusing highlights, not to mention a real problem solver.

Entertaining friends and family is my way of extolling the virtues of living happy and well in tight quarters, honing my skills as a confident, perfectly imperfect hostess. Where do you check in guests' coats and bags? In the bathtub, of course! Only twelve scrawny inches to spare for a bar? Transform a flea market chair into a pop-up pub, complete with a built-in ice bucket. If you can't hide it, celebrate "small" as a central theme of your party. Serve tiny bites and mini-cocktails. Entertaining in a small space is all about making lemon martinis out of lemons!

Here's the skinny on getting your party mojo up and running, even if you live in dinky digs:

Not That!

- 🍷 No one expects perfection. Your guests expect fun. You living it up at your own party sets the mood for everyone.

- 🍷 Invite a buddy to be your cohost for the night. There is comfort in numbers. Minimize the stress and share the joy.

- 🍷 Use what you have and repurpose rooms in unexpected ways—even the bathroom!

- 🍷 Mix things up! Feel free to pair plastic with crystal, paper with heirloom silver, homemade with store-bought. Let your personality shine through.

- 🍷 Focus on one wow factor: old movies projected onto the wall, a flaming cocktail, a DIY photo booth in a closet. It's about quality and originality, not quantity or size.

Guess what? Your name's been added to the top of the *Decorate This, Not That!* VIP list for time-saving, stress-free party tips with offbeat, posh party décor that is foldable, collapsible, storable, or repurposeable. Pop open a bottle of bubbly, and let's get this party started!

Entertain and designate a cramped corner as selfie central,

deprive guests of their social media fix.

Throwing a selfie-worthy party means providing a fun and colorful spot for the perfect group shot. Without an inch to spare, sometimes the only place is up on the sofa. Dressing up the curtains with paper flowers and balloons for an improvised backdrop is all a crowd needs to get snap happy.

Entertain and organize with a coat check in the bathtub, *not* toss dirty coats and bags onto a bed.

A sturdy folding wardrobe rack is narrow enough to set up inside a bathtub or shower and is a surprisingly affordable small-space essential you will use over and over again. Keep the look neat and chic with spray-painted gold hangers and custom coat-check tags. Also include baskets below to store heavier backpacks and larger bags. Just remind your guests at the end of the night: no tipping necessary!

Entertain and flip baskets into portable ice chests for the night, be a party buzzkill serving warm beer.

Ice wins best supporting role at every party, but when you entertain in a tiny nest with a junior-size fridge, it's nearly impossible to house enough champagne buckets and ice chests to keep a bash chillin'. Use baskets you might already have in your closet and tuck in foldable, insulated lunch bags for impromptu ice chests that really keep their cool.

tip 👉 *How much ice? Plan on at least one pound of ice per person per hour or one pound of ice per quart if you are filling up ice chests and champagne buckets. Set your timer for 30 to 45 minutes prior to guest arrival to put bottles on ice.*

tip 👉 *Chill wine in 15 minutes or less. Add a handful of salt and a cup of water to a bucket of ice. The water will create a larger cooling surface area, and salt speeds the drop in temperature.*

Entertain and convert a flea market chair into a pop-up, self-serve champagne bar,

not

be tethered to filling wine glasses all night.

Create the ideal party flow by staging self-serve bars in various corners of the apartment. By day, the dependable seatless flea market chair holds a sizable shoe collection in just one square foot of space. Switching gears to party mode is a cinch and only requires a repurposed basket to hold bottles of bubbly and a 12-inch plastic punch bowl for the ice that fits snugly inside the seat's frame. Champagne cork hooks hold hanging wine glasses at the ready for guests to use.

miy PROJECT

To make champagne cork hooks, screw in twelve 1-inch hanger bolts or dowel screws (ask for #8, 32-by-1-inch), which will hold a set of six glasses, around the sides of the chair. On the bottom center of each cork, poke a tiny pilot hole with a nail and twist the cork into the blunt end of the installed hanger bolt until it is flush with the frame of the chair. Hang champagne and wine glasses upside down between two cork hooks. Simple twine holds a hanging bubbly basket securely to the chair. Line the basket with an insulated freezer bag to keep extra bottles chilled.

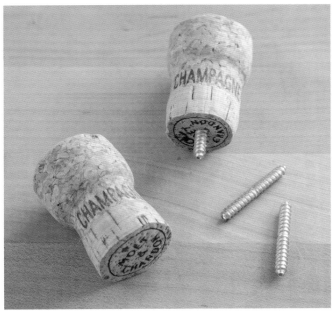

tip ☞ *To reduce condensation from the ice, use two bowls—one stacked on top of the other—with a dishcloth draped in between.*

Entertain and celebrate petite as the gimmick of the party, **not** go theme-less.

Turn your lack of real estate into a delightful "mini" party theme that keeps an event focused. Stock the bar with miniature liquor bottles, mini-tini cocktail glasses, and bite-size cones and ice cream sandwiches. Make sure to serve the tiny desserts on a bed of itty-bitty chocolate chips to put *big* smiles on your guests' faces.

Entertain and dazzle with personal touches,

be self-conscious about the cramped quarters.

When a soirée is short on inches, it's time to double up on personality and divert attention away from the space-challenged party venue. Put your individual stamp on wood bottle toppers that turn everyday water and juice bottles into festive help-yourself wine and spirit decanters.

*miy*PROJECT

Attach adhesive vinyl letters on a three- or four-inch wooden craft ball and spell out your initials or a cheeky saying. Use a paint stain pen (available in many shades) to color the entire ball, leaving the letters untouched. Let dry, then peel off the adhesive letters, and for further definition, outline the letters with a brown paint pen. Let dry for 24 hours before using.

Entertain and stock a dinky living room with folding snack and cocktail trays, *not* be codependent on cumbersome coffee tables.

These affordable plastic TV trays take up zero floor space and tuck under sofa cushions to hold snacks during movie night or cocktail hour. They disassemble and store flat as a pancake when not in use. Spray-paint yours in a bold color to coordinate with the party theme in a snap.

tip ☞ *For a smooth and durable finish, make sure to use a paint primer before spray-painting plastic. Line tray tops with whimsical paper placemats for easy post-party cleanup.*

Entertain and beef up cocktail table space with sofa arm tables you can make in a jiff, *not* pressure guests to juggle appetizers with their martinis.

For space-starved soirées, sofa arm tables that sneak into tight corners where you need them most keep cocktails and snacks securely on the edge of their seats. All it takes is a wooden cigar box and a bamboo sushi rolling mat. The sofa arm table stores away flat and out of sight until the next get-together.

miy PROJECT

Spray-paint a bamboo sushi mat a color to match your theme or décor. Paint the lid of a wooden tea or cigar box to match, and glue it onto the center of the mat for the ideal-sized cocktail tray. For added surface traction, use rubber foam stickers to spell out your favorite cocktail toast or sentiment on the top of the tray. Glue a nonslip rubber shelf liner onto the back of the sushi mat, which keeps it from sliding off the sofa arm. Place the mat and tray over a sofa arm, and poke a Tidy Pin (found at sewing notions stores) through the front of the mat to the back and into the sofa arm (two for each side). They are designed for upholstery and won't harm the fabric.

tip ☞ *Pre-spray furniture and rugs with Scotchgard to prevent stains. It will help repel unexpected wine and food stains.*

Decorate and wrap ice buckets with carpenter aprons for a self-serve beverage corner,

not

sweat the event like an overworked cocktail waitress.

For an instant cocktail/bar zone that is chic, clean, and compact, wrap a handy carpenter's apron (found at hardware stores) around an ice bucket and fill the five pockets with bottle openers, ice tongs, stirrers, and straws for impromptu get-togethers. Come cocktail hour, guests help themselves and mingle while the hostess is free to enjoy her own party.

tip ☞ *If your ice bucket has handles, create two large grommet holes so they can poke through. For extra durability, before cutting in the grommet hole, reinforce the area underneath with a small piece of fusible drapery header tape. Now the fabric is stiff enough to prevent fraying once the grommet ring is inserted.*

174

Entertain and feature a miy signature cocktail with a recipe voice recorder, *not* limit the bar to beer and wine.

A signature cocktail makes everyone feel like a VIP at a party and transforms the event into a grander affair, despite how pocket-sized the venue may be. Surprise your friends and leave a how-to cocktail recipe message on a greeting card voice recorder. A push-button style recorder works best. Cut a small hole in a plastic lemon or lime—just big enough to snugly fit the recorder—and display it on top of a bowl full of fresh citrus. Tie a tag that tells guests, "To Drink, Press Play."

miy RECIPE

Champagne Guava Mojito

In a short glass, muddle a handful of fresh mint leaves, 2 packets of sugar and the squeeze of half a lime. Add to a martini shaker. Mix 2 ounces white rum, a splash of Grand Marnier, and 2 ounces guava nectar into a martini shaker with ice, and shake. Strain and pour into a tall glass a little more than halfway, and top off with a crisp bubbly, like Le Grand Courtâge.

tips ☞ *To prevent bottlenecking at the food and beverage stations, place the* mix-it-yourself *signature cocktail bar in the opposite corner of the beer and wine table.*

How much alcohol to buy? For a typical three-hour-long cocktail party, estimate that each guest will drink an average of two drinks the first hour and one drink after that, and you'll be covered.

Entertain and swap out a few shelves in a TV cabinet for a one-night standing bar,

have guests crowd a cramped kitchen.

Look at your nutshell through wine-colored glasses and reclaim an ordinary TV armoire as a chic pop-up bar. To display stemware, extend two small café curtain tension rods across the width of the armoire, spread about three inches apart from each other. Slide in plastic stemware (avoid glass, which would be too heavy and not safe) between the two rods, hanging stem side up. For the bar menu, use white chalk ink pens on empty glass picture frames. Hello, happy hour!

tip ☞ Hang metal flowerpot holders from the dollar store securely on the armoire doors to cradle bottles of sparkling water. Spray-paint them gold for some extra shimmer.

Entertain and put a lazy-Susan cheese plate to work, *not* force guests to play elbow hockey at the buffet table.

Outfitted with a piece of chalkboard fabric cut to fit (available at any sewing supply store), a lazy Susan becomes the ultimate tabletop space saver. Use chalk to designate names of cheeses, and draw circles to divvy up plate placement to guarantee easy access to the entire platter. And when not working the room, the chalkboard fabric folds away, and the lazy Susan goes back into cupboards to organize spices.

Entertain and decorate with conversation starters, like a million-dollar floor plan placemat, predictable white tablecloths.

With an ironic nod to some of the most luxurious penthouses in the country, print floor plans (available for free online) onto placemats and napkins at your next small-space shindig. Use artist molding paste and a laser printer to transfer your images to a cotton placemat. (Refer to the "Lofty Living Room Dreams" chapter's fireplace slipcover MIY project.) Your guests will have fun figuring out where and who owns these multimillion-dollar homes.

Entertain and display party eats on temporary footed platters, *not* arrange food on boring trays.

tip 🖝 *Go easy on yourself. Make it a goal that 75 percent of your menu can be prepared in advance with minimal heating or assembling.*

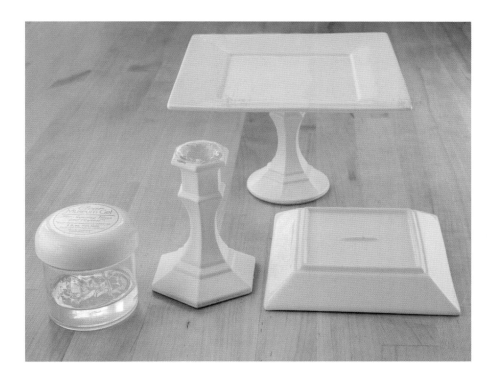

Footed cake stands maximize the vertical space on a tiny tabletop and are the *stilettos* of the party-catering world. Everything looks more appetizing and, frankly, a little sexier displayed up high. Also, the higher the platter, the grander your petite pad will appear to be. But trying to store footed platters in a cluttered cupboard is anything but sexy. Instead, regular plates, graduating in size, can be stacked to dramatic heights with eggcups or candlestick holders for makeshift footed platters for the night. The trick is to use removable (and reusable) Museum Gel, found at better kitchen and hardware stores, to keep the layers secure. When it's a wrap, plates disassemble in a snap.

tip ☞ *A party-in-a-nutshell can be a bit of a juggling act, quite literally, for guests trying to balance a glass of chardonnay with a plate full of hot appetizers. Ceramic cocktail mingling plates that hold a stem glass and tiny bites all in one are must-haves for your go-to party pantry. When it's not party season, use them as part of your everyday plate rotation.*

Entertain and blow up inflatable ottomans as fun, in-a-pinch guest seating,

not

pressure guests to squat on the floor.

When you think of inflatable furniture, flashbacks to a tacky college dorm might come to mind, but plastic blow-up ottomans, layered with a luxurious shearling throw, save the day as guest seating that is all grown up and ready to get the joint jumpin'! When it's time to say good-night, let the air out and easily store deflated ottomans without taking up premium shelf space behind closet doors.

tip ☞ *To keep the shearling throw from slipping and sliding around, drape a rubber no-slip shelf liner between the throw and the plastic ottoman.*

Entertain and bump up regular stools to cocktail table status, *not* run out of spots to rest a drink.

Proven time and time again, standing cocktail tables make the most of the least amount of party space. Use what you have and give counter stools (measuring 24 to 30 inches tall) a six-inch boost to comfortable cocktail bar height with clean plastic takeout food containers as chair risers. Cover the newly converted cocktail tables with a tablecloth that drapes to the floor and no one will be the wiser. Cheers!

Entertain and cast a glorious party glow with Mason-jar lights,

 not

leave messy candle wax behind.

The ubiquitous Ball Mason jar, lit with battery-operated LED lights, adds a festive glow sprinkled throughout your home, without fear of the party literally going down in flames. Play up the word ball, embossed on the front of the jar, with puffy stickers in a similar font, and spray-paint with the color of your choice.

tip ☞ *Set the mood and swap out regular light bulbs in your lamps with amber-colored ones that reflect the look of soft, romantic candlelight.*

tip ☛ Use both real and battery-operated candles for the party. Go with real candlelight for the center table, and flameless votive candles can fill in everywhere else. Battery-operated tea lights safely tuck into bookshelves, glass cabinets, along baseboards, stairs, and windowsills—little nooks where you would feel nervous using real flames.

tip ☛ For extra illumination, place round office adhesive labels (the thin plastic ones) along the bottom third of the jar. Spray-paint the entire jar metallic gold and remove the round sticker labels when completely dry. The unpainted glass "dots" will allow for more light to shine through. After the night comes to a close, jars go back to organizing office and craft supplies.

Entertain and celebrate the guest of honor with lampshade cutouts,

not

with tired banners and garlands.

Steal this Hollywood tip! Seasoned party planners use pricey lighting *gobos*, or cutout inserts made from metal or glass and placed in front of a spotlight to cast mood-enhancing shadows. Here's how to create the same effect for less: Snap a profile photo of the birthday girl. Print the image in black and white onto light cardstock and cut out the silhouette. Use ordinary transparent tape to adhere the cutout to the inside of the shade. Add die-cut "Happy Birthday" cardboard tiaras to complete the message. The paper cutouts are easily removed without harm to the lampshades, and the guest of honor will be thrilled to see her name and face in lights.

Entertain and improvise a cocktail table from an over-the-door ironing board,

not

spend money on a one-off party accessory.

Any diehard petite-party pro knows that if something is not nailed down, it is fair game to use at an event, even if that means delegating an ironing board to the night shift. For an extra cocktail table that can slide into a tight corner, over-the-door ironing boards are always *down* for a one-night stand. Dress up your new *pop-down* cocktail table with a piece of foam core that extends an inch or so longer than the ironing board. Then drape everything with a festive tablecloth. When the last guest leaves, the ironing board springs back into hiding.

Appendices

The patterns (opposite) can be used to replicate the design for the MIY curtain project found on page 25. Draw these patterns to the size of your choosing on pieces of freezer paper, and cut them out to create the stencils that will be used on your curtains. Next, place the newly constructed stencils on your curtains, and paint and fill the negative space around the stencils. Once it's dry, lift the freezer-paper stencils, leaving behind a white pattern. Your old curtains now have a fun, new design.

Stencil Patterns

Where to Buy

pg. 12:
Sherwin-Williams Rarified Air
Sherwin-Williams.com

pg. 20:
Annie Sloan Chalk Paint in
English Yellow
AnnieSloan.com

pg. 22:
Vintage Metal Tole Tray
Antique Addictions on **Etsy.com**

pg. 24:
Apple Barrel Paint in Kelly Green
Michaels.com

pg. 26:
X-Frame Over-the-Commode Etagère
Target.com

pg. 27:
Chair Caning
FrankSupply.com

pg. 29:
Anvandbar Cotton Fabric (on chaise)
Ikea.com

pg. 30:
Dahlia Wood Bead Chandelier
PotteryBarnKids.com

pg. 32:
Baxton Studio Acrylic End Table
Magazine Rack
Houzz.com

2 in. Clear Polyurethane Light Duty
Swivel Caster
HarborFreight.com

pg. 33:
GPS Custom Decal
Hour Glass Design Co. on **Etsy.com**

pg. 34:
Gold Fine Handmade Paper
PaperSource.com

pg. 36:
Artist Primed Canvas Rolls
DickBlick.com

pg. 37:
Medium Modeling Paste
Michaels.com

pg. 38:
Wooden Craft Sticks
Walmart.com

pg. 40:
Chicken of the Sea- Woman Holding
Tuna 1931
SanDiegoHistory.org

pg. 41:
Wood Wiggle Molding or Horizontal Wood
Closure Strips
HomeDepot.com

pg. 43:
Threshold Gold Bathroom Caddy
Target.com

pg. 45:
Gold Wood Tray
WestElm.com

pg. 48:
Clear Globe String Lights
Target.com

pg. 52:
Wood Lattice Molding Strips
Lowes.com

pg. 53:
Frogtape-Scallops
Walmart.com

pg. 54:
White Coin Flex Rubber Tiles
RubberFlooringInc.com

pg. 56:
Bistro Counter Chair
WorldMarket.com

pg. 60:
Krusning Pendant Lamp Shade
Ikea.com

Jute Rope Electrical Cord Swag Kit
WorldMarket.com

pg. 61:
Moroccan Scallops Wall Stencil
RoyalDesignStudio.com

pg. 64:
In the Garden-Giclee Art Print
Britney Jette on **Etsy.com**

pg. 66:
Beveled Square Frameless Wall Mirrors
Lowes.com

pg. 68:
Stockholm Blad Fabric
Ikea.com

pg. 70:
Grundtal Stainless Steel Shelf
Grundtal Dish Drainer
Ikea.com

pg. 71:
Marble Carrara Grey Contact Paper
DesignYourWall.com

pg. 73:
Marble Cheese Server
CB2.com

pg. 75:
Wood Painting Panel
ArtistCraftsman.com

pg. 79:
Wood Candle Cups
Joann.com

Marble Lazy Susan
BedBathandBeyond.com

pg. 86:
Sherwin-Williams Amazing Gray
Sherwin-Williams.com

pg. 117:
Duralee Blue White Lapis Chinoiserie
InsideFabric.com

pg. 118:
Tarno Wood Folding Café Chair
Ikea.com

pg. 121:
Young House Love Champagne Bronze
Vintage Style Bail Pull Set
HomeDepot.com

pg. 126:
Creatology Assorted Wood Shapes
Michaels.com

pg. 127:
Honey-Can-Do Wicker Corner Hamper
BedBathandBeyond.com

pg. 128:
Polyurethane
Corbel
VanDykes.com

pg. 129:
Teak Bathtub Caddy
BedBathandBeyond.com

pg. 132:
Vellum Paper
Staples.com

pg. 133:
Lamp Shade Clip-On Adapter
HomeDepot.com; **BedBathandBeyond.com**

pg. 134:
Chrome Towel Shelf & Bar
OrganizeIt.com

pg. 135:
12-Compartment Vanity Organizer with
Magnetic Strip by Threshold
Target.com

pg. 136:
Moroccan Floor Tile Decals
Bleucoin on Etsy.com

pg. 146:
Bamboo Wine Table
UncommonGoods.com

pg. 150:
Shapecrete-Moldable Cement Mix
HomeDepot.com

pg. 152:
Resin Outdoor Urns
TuesdayMorning.com

pg. 154:
Loopy Rubber Door Mat
Houzz.com

Live Moss
RiceWineDIY Shop on **Etsy.com**

pg. 156:
Venus Head Planter
OneKingsLane.com

Ceramic Llama Planter
WestElm.com

pg. 157:
Double Wood Picture Frame
Michaels.com

Bamboo Purse Handle
Joann.com

pg. 158:
Pom Juice Bottle
Walmart.com

Plant Nanny Terracotta Wine Bottle
Stakes
Amazon.com

pg. 163:
Love Script Rose Gold Balloon
PaperSource.com

pg. 166:
Le Grand Courtage Sparkling Wine
LeGrandCourtage.com

pg. 168:
Mini Liquor Bottles
WorldMarket.com

pg. 169:
Mini Cones and Ice Cream Sandwiches
TraderJoe.com

pg. 174:
CLC 5-Pocket Canvas Waist Apron
AceHardware.com

pg. 175:
Recordable Sound Module
Amazon.com

pg. 176:
Café Curtain Tension Rod
Walmart.com

pg. 177:
Addison Float Frame Gold by Threshold
Target.com

pg. 178:
Chalkboard Fabric
Joann.com

pg. 181:
Museum Gel
ContainerStore.com, Walmart.com

pg. 187:
Over-the-Door Ironing Board
Walmart.com

Index

U

V

W

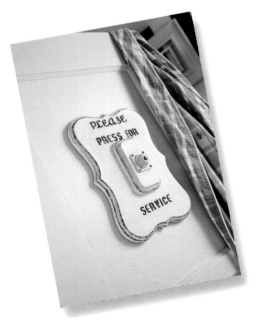

Acknowledgments

Now that the paint has dried and each room has been preserved as a snapshot in time, the words from the inimitable Gloria Vanderbilt ring truer than ever, that "decorating is autobiography." The yearlong transformation of this petite cottage begins to tell the story of a design life made rich and full by a cast of indelible characters.

Marta Hallett unleashed her superpower as editor and publisher when she gave this book idea a resounding yes. Her belief in the beauty of this project caused a sizable shift in the Earth's axis in my private universe, because when Marta believes in you, you begin to think you can leap tall buildings in a single bound. With the help of Gabrielle Schecker and the G Arts design team, *Decorate This, Not That!* started to come to life.

The book gods were smiling down on me when I found photographer Gail Owens, who channeled the spirit, whimsy, and soul of this cottage one square foot at a time, one frame at a time. Thank you for your artful eye. And much gratitude goes to graphic designer and friend Linda Stehno, whose sweet illustrations are the cherry on top of the gorgeous cake.

When this project was nothing but hopeful words on a page, Momina Khan carefully measured every sentence and comma. With her proofreading prowess, she gave me the first glimpse into the true potential of this book.

Writing and decorating can be solitary pursuits, and that's why the success of the book and the sanity of its author depended so heavily on the boundless faith and friendship of Cyd Upson and late-night calls to the ultimate optimist, Joseph Lecz. Tawnya Falkner, Ruben Galvan, Juan Villaneuva, and Amber Lichens, I knew I could count on you in a pinch!

A big thank-you goes to Joe Sinatra, a rock-star contractor who was always there on the sidelines to show me how to carry out my crazy design schemes or to talk me out of them when they are not the best way to proceed.

And Thomas H. Lee, who is the big brother you always dreamed of having in your cheering section. Thank you for taking no more than two seconds to say yes to this passion project and for happily becoming its sponsor.

To my first and forever friend, Donna Kirch. You are a soothsayer. You said there was a second book in me before I believed it. Thank you for always dreaming bigger and better—and in Technicolor—than I could ever do for myself.

Finally, dear Jin Hwa. Earning your joyful seal of approval on every project, fabric swatch, and paint sample, I knew we had a winner. Thanks to your keen design eye and your lifelong collection of vintage treasures that I happily pilfered for every room in this cottage, this book became precious. It is a lovely bonus that I can also call you mom. Sarang-hamnida.